$5 Million

In 8 Years

Real Estate

Investing on the Side

By David S. J. Meng

This book serves as a helpful tool on real estate investing. However, laws and regulations and situations often differ from place to place. The reader should seek the services of legal, accounting and financial professionals, as such services are not provided by this book. Real estate has been a proven and fruitful opportunity for numerous investors. However, any investing also has the possibility to lose money, and events such as economic changes and local market conditions are not the responsibility of this author. While the author and publisher have used their best efforts to prepare this book, they make no warranties regarding the accuracy or completeness of the contents of this book. The author and publisher bear no liability and the reader is responsible for his or her own investing failures and successes.

Dedication

To my parents, who despite extreme poverty raised three kids and sent us to college by their hard work and sacrifice. In memory of my father, who built houses for other people to support his family, and passed away on December 15, 2018.

Table of Contents

1. Introduction
2. Our First Rental Property
3. A Fixer Upper
4. An Emergency Settlement
5. A Condo Unit in an Office Building
6. An Entire Office Building
7. The Wonders of Compounding
8. Dare to Compare
9. Raising Funds and Networking
10. The What, When, and How in Buying Rental Properties
11. Building a Team
12. Other People's Time and My Emotional Detachment
13. Train Your Eyes to See Opportunities
14. Think Big
15. Pull the trigger, Take the Risk, and Manage the Risk
16. Courage, Resilience, and Optimism
17. Tell Me Where I'm Going to Die So I'll Never Go There
18. Better Late Than Never
19. Pursuing the Right Direction Is More Important Than Running Fast
20. Giving Back

Our Net Worth

Annual Rate of Return

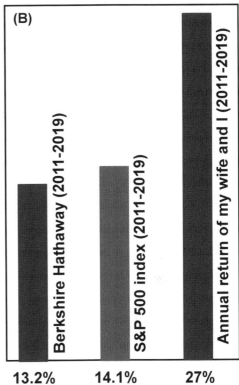

(A)

After almost two decades of jobs (1993-2011)

After 8 years of investment (2011-2019)

(B)

Berkshire Hathaway (2011-2019)

S&P 500 index (2011-2019)

Annual return of my wife and I (2011-2019)

$0.8 million $5.5 million   **13.2%   14.1%   27%**

(A) In 1993, my wife and I graduated and started working. We are ordinary employees, started from 0, and have had no inheritance. In 2011, we started to buy rental houses. We have full-time jobs and three kids, and we spent a few hours per week on real estate. Investing in real estate has made a big difference in our net worth. In addition, our net positive cash-flow from rental properties has approached $150,000 per year.

(B) Returns for Berkshire Hathaway (led by Mr. Warren Buffett, one of the best investors of all time) and SP 500 are obtained from https://www.berkshirehathaway.com/letters/2019ltr.pdf, which is gratefully acknowledged. The returns are averaged from 2011-2019, to be comparable to our time period of 2011-2019. The returns are compounded with dividends and profits reinvested. Small real estate investors can beat the market, compound wealth at a fast rate, and reach the dream of financial freedom. This book tells our true story and uses our real-life deals to show you how you can do it too.

About the author and this book. The author, David, was focused on his busy day job as a scientist. He came to the U.S. from China in 1988 as a student, graduated in 1993, started working and became a U.S. citizen. He and his wife have three kids born in the U.S. In 2010, their daughter's sudden sickness served as a wake-up call. It opened David's eyes to the fragility of an ordinary family's financial situation.

Since 2011, David and his wife, who are both full-time employees, have been investing in real estate on the side. With 50+ hours per week on his day job, David spent a few hours per week on real estate investing.

In eight years, they have increased their net wealth from $0.8 million to $5.5 million, at an average rate of 27% per year in net wealth accumulation. Their net positive cash-flow from rental properties reached $150,000 per year.

David wrote this book to empower you to achieve financial freedom too, regardless of your experience, just like how he started with little experience eight years ago.

Their investment experience is repeatable by others. This is not a "get-rich-quick" book by someone in a fast-growing local market which cannot be repeated by others in the long-term. David and his wife live in a normal market with housing price appreciation of 3-4% per year in the past eight years, similar to the long-term historic average in the U.S. David and his wife are ordinary working employees with 0 financial inheritance; quite the opposite, they send money to help parents and relatives. They send three kids to colleges with 0 student loans. They have expenses and financial responsibilities just like many other families.

Therefore, their investment experience and wealth accumulation, described in this book, are reproducible by others and sustainable in the long-term.

Through a series of true stories documenting his experience in real-life deals, David shares how you can spend a few hours per week on the side to begin to have your money work for you, and how you can obtain rates of return that far exceed those of mutual funds. This book will inspire you and show you how to reach your dream of financial freedom.

Chapter 1. Introduction

Now, one thing I tell everyone is learn about real estate. Repeat after me: real estate provides the highest returns, the greatest values and the least risk.

-- Armstrong Williams, entrepreneur

In June and July of 2010, my 15-year old daughter became sick and was in and out of the hospital for two weeks. We later learned that she had appendicitis, but she was initially misdiagnosed by the doctors, who told us that she probably ate something bad and would recover soon.

After two weeks, her condition suddenly worsened and she was sent to the emergency room in the middle of the night. She was hospitalized for three weeks from a ruptured appendix. The rupture created a life-threatening infection of her stomach.

Heavy antibiotics administered over two weeks failed to lower her temperature to normal. Finally, the doctors performed two procedures which successfully fought back the infection, and she gradually recovered. My wife and I stayed in the hospital with her every day for 21 days, during which my daughter lost more than 10 pounds and I lost 6 (and I had only 112 pounds to start with!).

It was during those heavy-hearted days that I realized I needed to do something for the family financially. Prior to that, as a scientist, I had focused only on my research and writing papers, and had not paid much attention to money. It dawned on me that if one of our children suddenly fell ill and became a long-term patient, my wife or I might have to quit our job to care for the patient. And if either one of us became a long-term patient ourselves, not only would the sick one be unable to work, but the other would have to compromise his/her job to take care of the spouse. Either scenario would mean a substantial reduction in income that would jeopardize the family finances.

The days with my daughter in the hospital were long, and I spent that time becoming increasingly determined to invest and secure the financial freedom for the family.

My daughter was finally discharged from the hospital and went home to recover. I called my real estate agent and told her that I would like to buy houses as rental properties, and that I planned to buy five houses.

I had read in a book that if you buy five houses as rentals and use the rent income to pay the mortgages every month, then after the mortgages are paid off, the rent income would be enough to live on. Then you would not have to work to earn a paycheck, and you have the option to quit your job. That would mean you have achieved financial freedom.

That was why I told my agent that I planned to buy five houses. My wife overheard the phone call and laughed. She thought that I was crazy to want to buy five houses. It's not like going to the supermarket and buying five bags of groceries. Five houses? We are a regular working family with ordinary income; where would the money come from?

We bought our first rental house in 2011. Eight years later, as of writing this book at the end of 2019, we have expanded to 14 rental properties.

Our net worth has increased from $0.8 million in 2011 (primary residence + retirement accounts) to $5.5 million in 2019 (mostly cash-producing properties). This represents an annual rate of 27% in our wealth accumulation.

The net positive cash-flow (after paying for mortgages, taxes, insurance, repairs, etc.) from our rental properties reached $150,000 per year.

My wife and I enjoy our jobs and have continued to work, but this cash-flow would be enough for us to live on if we chose to retire now.

In addition, (1) with gradual increases in rent, our cash-flow will increase over time. (2) Over the years to come, the mortgages will be gradually paid off, further increasing the cash-flow. (3) The values of the properties will continue to appreciate in the long-term. The situation is a win-win-win.

The draft of this book was finished near the end of 2019. During the Covid-19 shutdown, I had time to polish this book several times. As I checked with my real estate agent and Zillow.com in June 2020, the housing prices and rents in my area have continued to go up significantly. Therefore, our wealth has further increased and our investment return numbers quoted in this book are valid and conservative.

We have achieved this under relatively ordinary circumstances. As you'll see in the next chapters, we do not live in one of those booming, fast growing areas where real estate prices increase by 8% or 12% per year, enabling investors to "get rich quick". Such a "booming" may not be sustainable in the long-term, nor reproducible by you in your area.

Instead, the housing prices in our area have been increasing by a modest 3-4% per year in the past eight years, which is representative of a normal market and does not deviate significantly from the long-term historic average in the United States.

In addition, I am not a handy person who can do my own repair work on the houses to save money. My three lovely and talented kids tease me for calling a handyman to fix every small thing. Therefore, the aforementioned wealth accumulation was achieved through relatively normal appreciation by someone who is not particularly handy around a house – and I believe it is attainable for you too.

If you happen to be handy and can save money on house maintenance, or live in a faster-appreciating location, you could do even better.

Theodore Roosevelt once said: "Every person who invests in well-selected real estate in a growing section of a prosperous community adopts the surest and safest method of becoming independent, for real estate is the basis of wealth."

Indeed, compared to many other types of investments, real estate investing with a good and safe use of leverage, as this book will describe, can produce wonderful returns at a managed and minimized risk. As the famous entrepreneur Marshal Field put it: "Buying real estate is the best, safest way to become wealthy."

History shows that the majority of self-made millionaires made it through real estate.

According to the industrialist, business magnate, and philanthropist Andrew Carnegie: "Ninety percent of all millionaires become so through owning real estate. More money has been made in real estate than in all industrial investments combined. The wise young man or wage earner of today invests his money in real estate."

It is my hope that this book will inspire, encourage, and assist you in your pursuit of financial freedom.

Chapter 2. Our First Rental Property

The best investment on Earth is earth.

- Louis Glickman, real estate investor

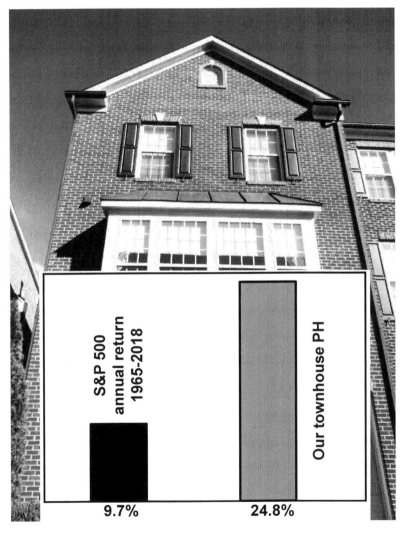

S&P 500 annual return 1965-2018: 9.7%

Our townhouse PH: 24.8%

My wife and I bought our first rental property in 2011. It was a three-story townhouse (referred to as house PH in this book). We settled on March 21, 2011 at a purchase price of $265,000. We put down 20%, and the rest was a bank loan. Now, for some math:

Down payment: $66,250. Closing costs: $13,317. Therefore, the total money that we threw into this house: $79,567.

The 30 year-fixed loan amount: $198,750.

Monthly mortgage payment: $1,516/month.

Principal reduction: $292/month.

The principal reduction amount can be understood as the amount that you pay into your own pocket. It is the amount that the loan is reduced by each month, because the monthly mortgage payment reduces the money you owe the bank. The principal reduction number gradually increases over time. While the monthly mortgage payment remains the same, the portion that goes to the principal increases and the portion that goes to the interest on the loan decreases over time.

Rent: $2,050/month. Therefore,

Positive cash flow = $2,050 (rent) − $1,516 (mortgage payment) − $100 (HOA dues) − $50 (repair) − $50 (vacancy) = $334/month.

Note: We bought rental properties in a good school area. In the past 8 years, this house has had a total vacancy of less than 1 month. We bought relatively new houses; house

PH was only 5 years old when we bought it, hence there was less need for repairs.

The housing price has been increasing slowly with time. According to zillow.com, the price estimate for house PH in 2019 was $379,889. Therefore, in the past 8 years, the price for house PH has increased from $265,000 to $379,889. This is how the price appreciation rate can be calculated: $379,889 / $265,000 = 1.046^8. This means that 1.046 - 1 = 0.046, which equals to 4.6%. The power ^{8} indicates the time period of 8 years. Hence, this yields an annual house price appreciation of approximately 4.6%.

Hence, the estimated house price appreciation in the first year (the first 12 months of appreciation) was $265,000 x 4.6% = $12,190. Then,

Annual rate of return for the first 12 months = (Net cash flow + principal reduction + house appreciation) / (Money we threw into this house)

Therefore, in the first 12 months, the rate of return = ($334x12 + $292x12 + $12,190)/$79,567 = 24.8%.

This is a simplified estimate, which one can do on the back of an envelope, to demonstrate the important point: With leverage, one can obtain a decent percentage of return on the invested capital, even if the housing price appreciated at only 4.6% annually. For example, the principal reduction was fixed at $292/month for simplicity; in reality, this number will become slightly bigger over time. The rent will also slowly increase over time after several years, which will increase the net cash-flow. The purpose here is not to provide an exact mathematical calculation of the rate of return, but rather, to illustrate a simple and straightforward estimate that you can perform on the back of an envelope when you are looking to buy a house. Whether or not you want to use complicated Excel spreadsheets and complex equations, whether the exact calculation would yield 24.8% or 23.9%, it does not affect the money that eventually goes into your pocket. My personal criteria is that, as long as the return is above 15%, it is a deal worth pursuing.

Also note that this is an estimate of the return for the first year. Returns for subsequent years will vary because the rent may be increasing, the principal reduction will increase, and the equity in the house will gradually increase.

The equity in the house refers to the difference between the house price and the remaining loan amount (equity = house value – remaining loan amount). After several years of appreciation and paying down the loan, the equity in the house will increase. Therefore, the rate of return on that equity will decrease:

Annual rate of return on the equity in the house = (Net cash flow per year + principal reduction per year + house appreciation per year)/Equity in the house.

The larger the equity in the house, the smaller the rate of return on that equity. However, you can do a cash-out refinance to pull some cash out.

For example, assume your house has appreciated to $400,000, and you owe the bank a mortgage of $150,000. That means that you have $250,000 equity in the house. In a cash-out refinance, the bank can give you a loan of, say, 75% of the house value. 75% x $400,000 = $300,000. Since you still owe the bank $150,000, your take-home cash is $300,000 - $150,000 = $150,000.

In this simple example, the closing costs are not included; you should consult with your loan officer on closing cost details. The emphasis here is that a cash-out refinance can reduce the equity in the house and increase your rate of return. You can then use this cash to buy another property.

The important point of this chapter is: With proper use of leverage, you can turn a rental house with an unexciting annual price appreciation of 4.6% into a lucrative investment at a return of 24.8% on the invested capital. Therefore, even if you live in a normal or slow-appreciating housing market, it is still possible to obtain a rate of return in your real estate investment that substantially exceeds the compound annual return rate of 9.7% for the S&P 500 index.

Chapter 3. A Fixer Upper

I often meet people who are too busy to take care of their wealth ... I believe that each of us has a financial genius within us. The problem is, our financial genius lies asleep.

-- Robert T. Kiyosaki, author of Rich Dad Poor Dad

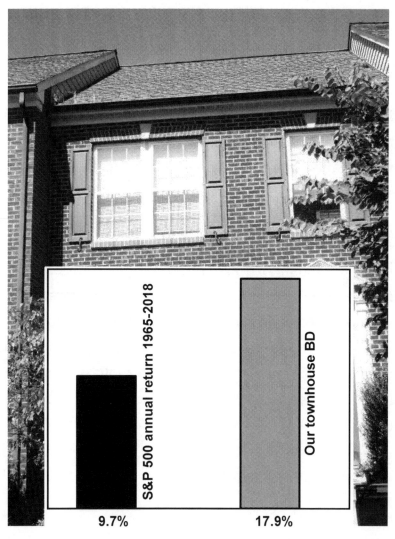

To avoid boring you, I will not describe every property that we bought. I will only describe a few typical deals with unique and important aspects that you will find helpful.

After buying three townhouses, we became bolder and bought a 4th with extensive damage in the basement. My go-to handyman helped hire a contractor to fix the basement and the rest of the house for $11,000. Because of the extensive damage in the basement, this house had difficulty securing a mortgage, so we paid a cash price of $241,000 to buy this house (referred to as house BD). The reason we bought it is that similar houses (without the damage) were selling for around $275,000. The damage looked bad and scared away other buyers, enabling us to get a very good deal. We settled in April 2012.

House price: $241,000. Closing costs: $12,410. Repair: $11,000. Thus, we threw a total of $264,410 into this house.

We later refinanced to pull out $125,000 cash. We would have liked to pull more cash out, but the lender would not allow us to take out more than $125,000. Therefore, the refinance means that we threw in a net of $264,410 - $125,000 = $139,410 into this house.

The 15-year fixed loan had a mortgage payment of $1,316/month.

Rent: $1,995/month.

Net positive cash flow = $1,995 (rent) − $1,316 (mortgage payment) − $100 (HOA dues) − $50 (repair) − $50 (vacancy) = $479.

(Note: We have had less than one month of vacancy in this house so far).

Principal reduction: $507.94 in the first month. As described in Chapter 2, this number gradually increases over time. For simplicity, I am fixing this number for the first year to estimate a rate of return. Just know that this is a simple and conservative estimate because this number slightly increases with time.

Regarding appreciation, Zillow estimate: $359,340 for this house in 2019. It has been 7 years. We paid $241,000 for this house but spent $11,000 on repairs. So, the effective purchase price in 2012 was $252,000. $359,340 / $252,000 = 1.052^7. This yields an annual appreciation rate of 5.2%.

Therefore, the estimated house pricing appreciation in the first 12 months was $252,000 x 5.2% = $13,104.

Rate of return in the first 12 months = (Net cash flow + principal reduction + house appreciation) / (Money we threw into this house) = ($479x12 + $507.94x12 + $13,104)/$13,9410 = 17.9%.

Note that this is lower than the rate of return for house PH. This was because we had thrown more cash into house BD, as the lender was too strict and would not allow us to borrow more.

Therefore, as long as you can break even on the house by using rent to pay all the expenses including mortgage and other costs, it is advantageous to obtain as big a loan from the lender as possible. The bigger the loan you can get from the lender, the less you will have to invest your own money into the house, and the higher your rate of return on the invested capital.

Nonetheless, an annual return of 17.9% is still excellent and far exceeds the long-term compounding return rate of 9.7% for the S&P 500 index. Furthermore, I have found a lender who is willing to lend us more money, and I am considering a cash-out refinance to pull more cash out to further increase the return rate.

The important points of this chapter are: (1) Do not let some damages or dirt in the house discourage you, because sometimes you can get a really good deal; (2) as long as you can break even, use as much of the lender's money as possible. This will enable you to obtain a higher rate of return on your invested capital, and the money that you do not have stuck in this house can be used toward the purchase of your next property.

Chapter 4. An Emergency Settlement

Don't wait to buy real estate. Buy real estate and wait.

-- Will Rogers, actor

We almost lost this house, referred to as PS. It's a townhouse for short-sale, because the owner (a young lady)

failed to make mortgage payments to her lender. We submitted an offer of $271,000, which was accepted by the seller. The offer, along with a bunch of supporting documents, were then submitted to the seller's lender for approval. After a few months, the lender approved our offer.

However, the seller's real estate agent (who worked with the lender's lawyer) suddenly demanded that we complete the settlement in two weeks. Typically, we would have 30-40 days to close the deal, which would give us enough time for our mortgage company to process the paperwork and approve our loan. However, in this case, according to our agent (the buyer's agent), the seller's agent had probably received another offer, after our offer had been submitted to the seller's lender. That other offer likely was a cash offer from a buyer who could close quickly. And that other buyer likely approached the seller's agent directly, meaning that the seller's agent would get the entire commission if that deal worked out. In contrast, if the house was sold to us, as was originally submitted, then the seller's agent would have to split the commission with my agent.

So, the seller's agent demanded that we close in two weeks, knowing that we needed to obtain a loan which would reasonably take about a month. When our agent asked for an extension for the settlement, he refused and blamed us for being too slow. It was apparent that he wanted us to walk away from this deal, so that he could sell this house to the other cash buyer and pocket the entire commission.

I enjoy running inside my house for exercise. I run from the family room to the library, through the sunroom, back to the family room, and so on, in circles for about an hour. I can never use the excuse that it's raining outside, or too hot, or too cold, to get out of exercising. That evening, I ran and thought about how to raise the $277,493 (the house price + closing costs) needed to close this deal. We had about $90,000 in the bank, enough for the 20% down payment and closing costs, as we had planned to obtain an 80% mortgage on this house. But now that we had only two weeks to close, there was no time to get a mortgage, and it was going to have to be a cash deal.

Suddenly, I remembered that years ago, we had saved money for children's tuitions in 529 plans. The 529 funds were appreciating slowly, at a rate of a few percentage points per year. I asked myself:

"Why don't we sell the 529 funds, and pay cash for this house? If I can make 20% per year investing on my own, why let someone else manage these funds at a hefty fee, while making only, say, 6% per year?"

The next day, I looked into our 529 plan's policies and happily found that there was no penalty in selling, except that we had to pay taxes on the appreciated amount, which was small anyway. We promptly sold these funds, and used the proceeds to close on the house, with cash, before the deadline. Needless to say, the seller's agent was disappointed that he did not pocket the whole commission. But my agent was happy that she got paid, and we were delighted that we got another house.

We then did a cash-out refinance on this house to pull money out to buy more properties. We pulled out $232,500, using a 30-year fixed mortgage. Therefore, the money that we threw into this house was $277,493 - $232,500 = $44,993.

Rent = $1,995/month.

Mortgage payment was $1,596/month.

Monthly positive cash flow in the first year = $1,995 (rent) − $1,596 (mortgage payment) − $100 (HOA dues) − $50 (repair) − $50 (vacancy) = $199/month. Note that when one pulls more money out, the cash flow is reduced.

Principal reduction: $352.50 in the first month. This number gradually increases over time as the principal portion in the mortgage payment gets bigger, while the interest portion becomes smaller over time. For simplicity, the principal reduction in the first 12 months is conservatively and simply estimated to be approximately $352.50 x 12 = $4,230.

For the house price appreciation, www.zillow.com estimated $359,081 for this house (2019). There were 6 years from 2013 to 2019. $359,081 / $271,000 = 1.048^6. This yields an annual appreciation of 4.8%.

Therefore, in the first 12 months after the cash-out refinance, the estimated house pricing appreciation in the first 12 months was $271,000 x 4.8% = $13,008.

Rate of return in these 12 months = (Net cash flow + principal reduction + house appreciation) / (Money we threw into this house) = ($199x12 + $4,230 + $13,008)/$44,993 = 43.6%.

The reason that this house had such a huge rate of return was that the lender allowed us to pull out a large amount of cash, so we only had a small amount of our own money invested in this house.

This rate certainly far exceeded what our 529 plan had been generating, and the pulled-out cash enabled further purchases of more townhouses. Our first child started college in 2013, our second child in 2016, and our third child in 2018. Using our salaries and cash-flow from the rental properties, we have been able to cover their college expenses so that they have 0 student loan debt. So we can rest easy that the selling of the 529 funds did not adversely affect our children's college education.

Of course, you will have to compare the rates of return and consider your own situation when making similar decisions. You may consult with your tax accountant or other related professionals if necessary.

The important point of this chapter is: Sometimes, you have to be creative and think outside the box in order to avoid losing a good deal. Be unconventional. Be courageous. Be persistent. In addition, it pays to control your emotions when you feel that you're being dealt with unfairly, and not let a rude agent anger you into walking away and losing a good deal. The rudeness of others should cost them; it should not cost you.

Chapter 5. A Condo Unit in an Office Building

Go confidently in the direction of your dreams! Live the life you've imagined.

-- Henry David Thoreau, essayist, poet, and philosopher

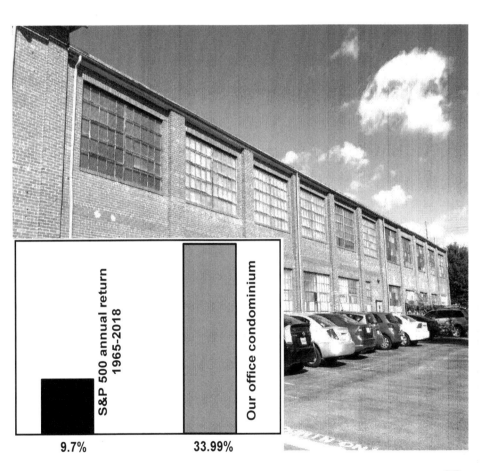

S&P 500 annual return 1965-2018: 9.7%

Our office condominium: 33.99%

In 2015, I was introduced to a gentleman who had done very well in real estate investing; let's call him Mr. LK. LK was a true gentleman, kind and generous and willing to teach and give advices. I invited him to dinner and we connected as friends.

LK was in his 70s and had invested in real estate successfully for many decades. Then, in 2017, he told me that his cancer had returned, and he would like to sell an office property that he owned. Fortunately, LK received advanced medical treatments and, as of polishing this book in June 2020, LK is still doing well. I wish him the best and many more healthy years to come. I spoke with a friend about the matter and we formed a 50/50 partnership, established a limited liability company (LLC), and bought this office property. We settled in September 2017.

This property is a condo (condo refers to condominium) in an office building, which includes other condos with other owners. Each condo pays a monthly fee to cover management costs and the maintenance of common areas, the roof, and the parking lot.

The condo that we bought had about 14,000 square feet of space, which was about a third of the entire building. The purchase price was $1.9 million. We obtained an 80% loan of $1.52 million. The 20% down payment plus closing costs amounted to $430,888, which we paid at settlement.

This condo unit was rented to a company, and we took over the lease, which was a triple-net lease. A triple net or "nnn" lease means that the tenant is responsible for paying real estate taxes, tenant's insurance and utilities, and tenant's repairs and maintenance. In the first year:

Rent: $15,965/month. Condo fee: $2,473/month. Our liability and umbrella insurance: $1,782/year.

Therefore, the cap rate = net rental income/the price of the building = ($15,965x12 - $2,473x12 - $1,782)/1,900,000 = 8.43%.

The cap rate is the rate of return assuming if the buyer pays with cash to buy the property, without using a loan. The rate of return can be increased with the use of leverage.

Our loan: 5-year maturity with 20-year amortization. Commercial loans usually do not have 15-year fixed or 30-year fixed types of loans, as residential loans do.

Our monthly mortgage payment: $8,634.85. Of this amount, $2,744.85 is for principal payment, and $5,890.00 is for interest, for the first month. The principal portion gradually increases with time while the interest portion decreases. For simplicity, the principal reduction in the first 12 months was approximately $2,744.85x12 = $32,938.20.

Net cash flow in the first 12 months = rent − condo fee − insurance − mortgage = $15,965x12 - $2,473x12 - $1,782 - $8,634.85x12 = $56,504.

The rent increase that was agreed upon in the lease was 3% per year. The price of a commercial property is usually related to the rent income that the property generates. Therefore, we assume that the property's price appreciation will also be 3% per year. This means an increase of $1,900,000 x 3% = $57,000 in the first 12 months.

Therefore, our rate of return in the first year = (Net cash flow + principal reduction + property appreciation) / (Money we threw into this property) = ($56,504 + $32,938.20 + $57,000)/$430,888 = 33.99%.

This is an outstanding rate of return. However, it should be noted that, as with other commercial real estate properties, if the current tenant company ever moves out, we will likely need to remodel to meet the needs of the new tenant. Or, we may need to subdivide the 14,000 square feet space into 2-3 units to rent to several companies that need smaller spaces. These factors would mean significant capital investment into the property, in addition to the rent lost before the new tenants would move in.

Office tenants are often long-term. For example, the current tenant has been there for twenty years (renting from LK), and has told us that his company has no plan to move out in the nearly future.

The important points of this chapter are: (1) Build connections and contacts, as sometimes good deals happen through these channels. (2) The LK deal demonstrates the important point that with careful leverage, it is possible to turn an 8% cap rate property into an investment with a 34% rate of return on the invested capital.

Chapter 6. An Entire Office Building

A pessimist sees the difficulty in every opportunity; an optimist sees the opportunity in every difficulty.

-- Winston Churchill

Mr. LK used his real estate agent NJ to close the deal with us. Then in early 2018, NJ brought another deal to our attention - an office building not far from the LK property.

This office building was built in 2004 by a prominent family developer in our region. The father who built this company was retiring, and his sons were taking over the company. The company was doing very well building luxury single family houses. They wanted to sell their office building so that they could use the proceeds to focus on buying land and building residential houses.

I went to visit this office building with NJ and had a meeting with one of the sons, John. I was happy to find that John seemed to be a decent and fair person.

The office building had 26,000 square feet of rentable space on a 2.2-acre land having a nice green lawn, with a large parking lot having 108 parking spots.

The numbers made sense. I liked this property. With several friends, we formed another LLC and bought this property. My wife and I have a 20.1% share in this property. We settled in July 2018.

The purchase price was $4.5 million. We took a loan of $3,600,000, which was 80% of the purchase price. The rest we paid with cash.

Our office building purchased via partnership

The loan has 7-year maturity with 25-year amortization. The monthly mortgage payment was $20,146.28. The first month's mortgage payment consisted of $13,950 in interest and $6,196.28 in principal.

The total annual rent was $638,337, rented to nine companies. The leases have a clause with a 3% annual increase in rent. Since the commercial property value is related to the rent income, this implies that the building price also increases at 3% annually.

This building does not have a condo structure, and we hired a management company to manage this property at a 5% management fee. The cap rate is similar to that of the LK property described in the last chapter. The rate of return on the invested capital for this building is also excellent and similar to that of the LK property as described in the last chapter, hence the math is not repeated here.

Instead, I would like to summarize my experience in the past years with residential houses and commercial properties, to aid you in deciding which type(s) of properties to invest in.

Thoughts on residential houses (including townhouses, detached single family homes and residential condos too). One advantage of residential houses as rental properties is that it is easier to find tenants for them than for office buildings if the office building goes vacant. If you have a vacant house, you can usually find tenants to fill it if you lower the rent by perhaps $50 or $100 per month below the market.

Another advantage of houses is that as long as you meet the lender's requirements, you can qualify for 30-year-fixed or 15-year-fixed interest loans. Commercial loans usually have a slightly higher interest rate and are fixed for a shorter period of 5-7 years.

Another advantage is that when the current tenant moves out and before the new tenant moves in, the landlord usually only needs to have the house cleaned and maybe the walls painted, in most cases without having to do major remodeling. However, significant remodeling is usually needed in an office property to suit the next tenant company.

On the other hand, a disadvantage of houses as rental properties is that it is more management-intensive, and if you want to find a management company to manage your townhouses or single houses, you will likely have to pay about 8% to 10% management fees. With our office building, the management fee is 5%. This is because the $4.5 million building is at one location under one roof. If you buy $4.5 million worth of townhouses, for example, you likely will have about a dozen or more townhouses at a dozen different locations with a dozen roofs, which would take more time and effort to manage.

Another disadvantage of houses is related to how long the tenants stay. In my townhouses, some tenants stay for one year, some have stayed for 5-6 years. The average is probably about 3 years. In office buildings, tenants usually stay longer, maybe up to 10 years or even 20 years. For example, in the LK office condo, the same tenant company has been there for more than 20 years.

Thoughts on office properties. Advantages of office buildings include simpler management and potentially long-term leases if the tenant company is doing well, as mentioned above. In addition, another advantage is that it is possible to find office buildings with a higher cap rate than that of a townhouse.

Furthermore, another advantage is that if you continue to grow as an investor, it is easier to scale up by investing in office buildings. For example, you may eventually scale up to own several office buildings worth a total of $30 million, consisting of, say, 10 office buildings worth $3 million each. You could still manage 10 office buildings. However, if you want to scale up to $30 million in townhouses, you likely will have around 100 townhouses, which would be quite difficult to manage.

A main disadvantage of office properties is that if the tenants move out, the offices may remain vacant for a long time. I have seen office buildings that stay vacant for months, sometimes several years. Then if you find a new tenant, you likely will need to pour in capital to divide or remodel the space to fit the needs of the new tenant company.

Thoughts on apartment buildings. For apartment buildings, vacancy is less of a concern as people will always need a place to live in. As long as you are willing to lower the rent to slightly below the market rate for comparable units, you should be able to find tenants.

Another advantage is that you usually only need to do cleaning and touch-ups before new tenant moves in. Possibly due to these advantages, the cap rates for apartment buildings may be lower than those for office buildings.

However, apartment buildings are management-intensive. Depending on the size of the building, an on-site full-time manager may be needed. Another potential disadvantage is that apartment buildings have a high density of people, which sometimes can mean loud noises, complaints, arguments and other issues.

Make selections with safe-guards. As an investor, you can do well in each category of rental properties. You do need to know how to evaluate the properties and to avoid buying at the top after many years of fast price appreciations.

My method for safeguarding investment in townhouses in my area is: If I make a 20% down payment, the rent income should at least offset the mortgage payment and all other expenses. In other words, the rent income should allow me to at least break even, and preferably, produce a small positive cash-flow. If I cannot at least breakeven, then I walk away. It means that the price is proportionately too high when compared to the rent. This helps avoid the risk of paying too much for the house, or getting caught up in bidding wars at the top during an euphoria.

You may live in a fast-growing area where houses are expensive and positive cash-flow is not possible with 20% down payment. Those areas rely mainly on appreciation, instead of cash-flow, to accumulate wealth. In those areas, you can either increase your down payment to break even, or tolerate a small negative cash-flow if you have a job with good income. After a few years, with rent increases, you will reach the point of break-even. After more time, you will then achieve positive cash-flow. It is important, though, to avoid buying rental houses at the peak of the housing cycle, which is especially important in fast price-appreciating areas.

On the other hand, my safeguard for office property is: If we put down 20%, we must have significant positive cash-flow after paying the mortgage and all other expenses. The significant positive cash-flow is to cover the risk of possible vacancies and remodeling expenses to fit the need of new tenants in the future. For example, the LK property generates an annual net positive cash-flow of approximately $56,504.

With a 20% down payment, breaking even may be fine for my townhouses in my area, but it is not good enough for an office property due to the possible risk of long-term vacancies and remodeling costs.

Indeed, in the past several years, there have been many townhouses and commercial real estate deals that we have looked at but walked away from. Either the cap rate was not high enough, or the location was a little too remote, or the whole office building was occupied by a single tenant (which could be a major problem if the tenant leaves). In several other potential deals, we walked away from a retail shopping center that could be pressured by online competition, and a restaurant that could be squeezed by the current wave of increasing minimum wages.

In commercial real estate, your profit is only as healthy as that of the companies who rent your spaces. Therefore, a company, a store, or a restaurant may close its door or declare bankruptcy if the business becomes bad. In such a case, you, the landlord, will likely not be able to enforce the nice long-term lease that you have signed.

As Mr. Warren Buffett, who has a good sense of humor, would say that some of his best actions were just sitting on his ass and doing nothing. Indeed, sometimes, you will just have to walk away from a deal, and the inaction may be the best action.

Now you have seen some of our real-life examples. Our rates of return ranged from approximately 17.9% to 43.6% in these properties. How important is the rate of return when you invest? This will be described in the next chapter.

Chapter 7. The Wonders of Compounding

Compound interest is the eighth wonder of the world. He who understands it earns it... he who doesn't... pays it.

-- Albert Einstein

The S&P 500 annual compound rate of return is 9.7% (1965-2018, dividend reinvested).

From 1965 to 2018, the famous Warren Buffett achieved an average annual return rate of 18.7%.

Ever since my wife and I started investing in real estate 8 years ago, our annual rate has been 27%.

Two questions:

(1) How important is this rate of return?

(2) How do we small investors achieve returns that beat the market?

The next two chapters discuss question 1. Then the subsequent chapters focus on question 2.

Albert Einstein once said that compound interest is the 8th wonder of the world. Indeed, increasing the rate of return by a few percentage points makes a huge difference, through the power of compounding interest, as you will see in the following examples.

Example 1: Assume that you invest $100,000 (If you invest $10,000 instead of $100,000, then please just reduce the following $ numbers by a factor of 10). At a 7.2% annual rate of return (Note: the annual returns in this book are compound rate with dividend and profits reinvested), your money will double every 10 years (M = million):

Year 0	Year 10	Year 20	Year 30	Year 40
$100,000	$200,000	$400,000	$800,000	$1.6 M

The rule of 72: The amount of time required to double your money equals 72 divided by your rate of return.

For example, if the annual rate of return is 7.2%, then $72/7.2 = 10$. So, the money doubles every 10 years.

This can be confirmed with the equation: $1.072^{10} = 2$ (2 means that your money is doubled). The number 1.072 is from $1 + 7.2\% = 1.072$. The power ^{10} indicates 10 years.

Here are some other examples. If you invest your money at an annual return rate of 8%, then you will double your money every 9 years ($72/8 = 9$).

If you invest your money at an annual return rate of 12%, then you will double every 6 years ($72/12 = 6$).

If you invest your money at an annual return rate of 24%, then you will double every 3 years (72/24 = 3). The higher the rate of return, the faster you double your money.

Example 2: Use the same 40 years as in Example 1. At 10% return compounding per year, a $100,000 investment will become $100,000 x 1.10^{40} = $4.5 million at 40 years.

Example 3: At 15% return/year, a $100,000 investment will become $100,000 x 1.15^{40} = $26.8 million at 40 years.

In Example 3, if you make a one-time investment of $100,000 at the age of 30, it will become $26.8 million when you are 70. Of course, if you continue to invest more money in subsequent years, you will accumulate even more wealth.

Example 4: At an even higher 20% return/year, after 40 years, a $100,000 investment will become $100,000 x 1.2^{40} = $147.0 million. (If you invest $10,000, then it will become $14.7 million after 40 years.)

Compare Example 4 ($147 million) with Example 2 ($4.5 million), and you see the importance of the return rate. This is the difference between a good return (10%) and an excellent return (20%). If you double the rate from 10% to 20%, you do not just double your money from $4.5 million to $9 million; you increase it from $4.5 million to $147 million.

The important points in this Chapter. If you invest $10k instead of $100k, then just reduce the $ number by a factor of 10. The purpose here is not the absolute numbers. You can change the invested dollar number to suit your own situation. The numbers are only used to illustrate the two important and dramatic points in this Chapter: (1) the rate of return, and (2) holding for the long-term.

Wealth Accumulation in 40 Years

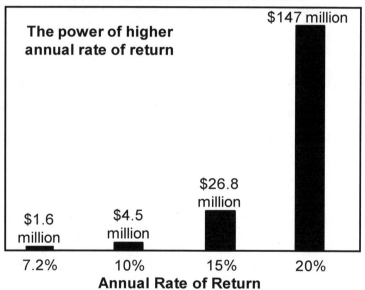

(Assume $100k initial investment, and profits are reinvested)

Why do most people fail to accumulate several million dollars after working for 30 or 40 years, even if they did save $10,000 to invest, or save $100,000 to invest? The key is the rate of return. For example, investing in a mediocre mutual fund that charges hefty annual fees would substantially slow down the wealth accumulation.

42

Therefore, the rate of return is critically important; it determines the potency of your compounding. Compounding is important, but compounding at what rate, and for how many years, are equally important.

Whether you invest in real estate or the stock market, or whether you select mutual funds for your retirement plans, focus like a laser beam on the annual rate of return. Do not let fancy mutual fund advertisements and marketing materials blur your focus on the net annual rate of return after all fees.

Wealth Accumulation at 20% Annual Return

(Assume $100k initial investment, and profits are reinvested)

As mentioned earlier, the second important point is how long you keep the investment, and how persistent you are in holding the investment to give it time to grow.

For example, at 20% annual return, if you invest $100k at the age of 27 (k = 1000), hold for 30 years and cash out the investment at the age of 57, you get $23.7 million. However, if you hold the investment for 10 more years and cash out at the age of 67, you get $147 million.

If these numbers look too big for you, remind yourself to think big. If you start early (say, around 25-35 years of age), and invest, say, at about 20% annual rate of return using the methods described in this book, these numbers are within reach.

If you invest $10k instead of $100k, then just reduce the $ numbers by a factor of 10 in these examples.

Of course, investment profits will have tax issues. One advantage of real estate investing is that it is tax friendly. Tax issues are not the focus of this book; for more information please consult with your tax accountant.

Key point: Strive to achieve relatively high rates of return, hold for many years, and you will witness the 8th wonder of the world.

Chapter 8. Dare To Compare

The KISS principle: "Keep It Simple, Stupid." ... If the opportunity is too complex and I do not understand the investment, I don't do it. Simple math and common sense is all that is needed to do well financially.

-- Robert T. Kiyosaki

There are many types of investments. They are often complicated; for example, various mutual funds cite different parameters and various numbers. As a small investor, we should keep it simple, focus on the annual rate of return, and compare the various investments by their rates of return. That's where the rubber meets the road, and that is what helps you accumulate wealth.

For example, many people invest in stocks and mutual funds. Employees have 401k or other retirement plans which are usually invested in mutual funds. Passive investing has become popular, and the S&P 500 index is one of the most commonly-followed equity indices. The S&P 500 is a stock market index that tracks the performances of the 500 largest companies listed on stock exchanges in the U.S. It is one of the best representations of the U.S. stock market.

The S&P 500 compound rate of return, with dividends included and reinvested, has averaged 9.7% annually from 1965-2018 (according to the Berkshire Hathaway 2018 annual report). Of course, there are ups and downs, with some years increasing by more than 30% and other times dropping more than 30%. But the average annual return in over half a century has been about 9.7% per year.

How do Wall Street investors and fund managers compare to the S&P 500 index? Mr. Warren Buffett, Chairman and CEO of Berkshire Hathaway, is one of the best and wealthiest investors of all time. The Berkshire Hathaway 2018 annual report shows an average annual return of 18.7% from 1965-2018.

This is an amazing and unparalleled achievement. $10,000 invested with Buffett in the beginning of 1965 becomes in 2018: $10,000 x 1.187^{54} = 100.5 million.

It should be noted that Mr. Buffett's returns have decreased as the company has grown larger. As Buffett said, he is not as nimble as he was in his earlier days when he had less money to invest. While his average annual return was 18.7% from 1965-2018, it has decreased in the last quarter century (1994-2018) to 14.34%. More recently, his annual return in the past 10 years (2009-2018) has further decreased to 11.88%.

Although Buffett's returns have moderated recently, he is still one of the best investors in history. He has become one of the top wealthiest people in the world through investing, an achievement few can obtain. Therefore, people can and should study him and learn a lot from him.

How do other fund managers fare? Mr. Buffett made a famous bet with hedge funds. In 2007, Buffett bet $1 million that an index fund such as the S&P 500 would outperform a basket of hedge funds, over a long-term period, such as a decade. Mr. Buffett chose the Vanguard's S&P 500 Admiral fund (VFIAX). Asset manager Protégé Partners selected a basket of funds of hedge funds. From 2007 through the end of 2016, Mr. Buffett's S&P 500 index fund returned an annual average of 7.1%. The competing basket of hedge funds returned an average of 2.2% annually. So Buffett won the bet handily, and the proceeds went to his chosen charity.

Granted, fund managers are highly intelligent people. They charge hefty fees. They are highly competitive and hard-working professionals. But the reality is that the majority of fund managers underperform when compared to the long-term return of the S&P 500 index.

Some funds may make a bet and win big in a year or two, but it is a very difficult task to consistently beat the S&P 500 over the long-term.

Indeed, according to the report with statistical numbers from the http://www.aei.org/publication/more-evidence-that-its-very-hard-to-beat-the-market-over-time-95-of-financial-professionals-cant-do-it:

"Over the 15-year investment horizon, 92.33% of large-cap managers, 94.81% of mid-cap managers, and 95.73% of small-cap managers, failed to outperform" their respective benchmarks.

For large companies specifically (since the S&P 500 represents large companies), according to the report of https://www.cnbc.com/2019/03/15/active-fund-managers-trail-the-sp-500-for-the-ninth-year-in-a-row-in-triumph-for-indexing.html:

"After 10 years, 85 percent of large cap funds underperformed the S&P 500, and after 15 years, nearly 92 percent are trailing the (S&P 500) index."

Therefore, if you pick stocks by yourself and you can match the compound annual return of 9.7% of the S&P 500 in the long-term, you are already ranked in the top 8% of all the large cap fund managers. Furthermore, if you can achieve a long-term compound annual return of 14% in the stock market, you are matching "The Buffett" of the past quarter century.

Indeed, if you can pick stocks and consistently outperform the S&P 500 in the long-term, you would be a Wall Street star, and the investment companies would be competing to hire you.

Mr. Buffett's long-term return of 18.7% made him the most famous investor in the world. Another top-notch investor, Sir John Templeton, is known for his famous advice: "Bull markets are born on pessimism, grow on skepticism, mature on optimism, and die on euphoria. The time of maximum pessimism is the best time to buy, and the time of maximum optimism is the best time to sell." His investment return over a span of 40 years was approximately 14% annually. Do not look down on 14% per year; it is a rare achievement, and Templeton is an investment legend.

Indeed, according to the report from the https://www.thebalance.com/good-annual-mutual-fund-return-4767418: A "good" long-term return (annualized, for a period of 10 years or more) is 8%-10% per year for stock mutual funds. (I am using the middle point 9% in the figure here). For bond mutual funds, a good long-term return is 4%-5% annually. Certainly, the poor funds would do much worse than these numbers. The various returns are shown in the figure.

Average Annual Rate of Return for Various Investments

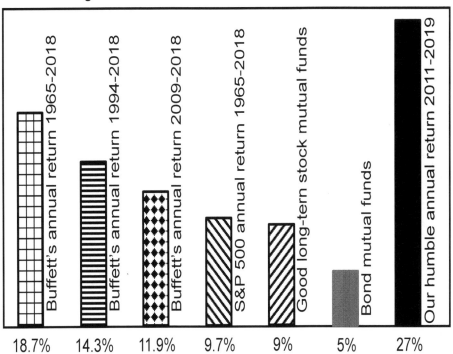

| 18.7% | 14.3% | 11.9% | 9.7% | 9% | 5% | 27% |

The return numbers on the x-axis are average annual compound returns, with dividend and profits reinvested.

In contrast, in real estate, with leverage, it is quite feasible to achieve return rates above 14% per year, sometimes even above 20% or 25%. You have seen some humble but real-life examples in this book.

In our case, from $0.8 million to $5.5 million in 8 years, $5.5/0.8 = 1.27^8$. Therefore, our annual rate is 27%.

Why can small real estate investors beat the stock market? If I compete with Mr. Buffett in analyzing the businesses and management qualities of companies to invest in the stock market, he will easily beat me. If I compete with other investors in selecting stocks, it is difficult, if not impossible, to beat the hundreds of professionals who do it full-time, have a team of analysts, and who visit the companies and play golf with the CEOs.

Therefore, in a competition to select stocks, I would be ranked not the best, nor the 2nd, nor the 3rd, but instead, the 10,000th, or worse. It is a tough battle to select stocks and consistently outperform in the long-term. Most mutual funds underperform the SP 500 index. That is why for my 401k retirement account, I simply put 100% of my money in a S&P 500 index fund, which charges a very low fee of 0.04%.

However, if you focus on real estate investing in your own neighborhood, Buffett is not coming to your neighborhood to invest in townhouses to compete with you. George Soros is not coming to compete with you, and Peter Lynch is not coming to compete with you.

You can become a true expert in your own backyard. You can possess a competitive edge within a few miles from where you live. That is why a small real estate investor can achieve very good rates of return.

The preceding two chapters show the wonder of compounding, and that an annual return rate of 15% to 20% or greater is really powerful in accumulating wealth. How did my wife and I achieve an average annual rate of 27%? How can small real estate investors beat the market? What does it take to be successful in real estate investing? These topics are the focuses of the next several chapters.

Chapter 9. Raising Funds and Networking

I use debt to buy assets. Most people use debt to buy toys and liabilities.

-- Robert T. Kiyosaki

As shown in earlier chapters on our real-life real estate deals, the proper use of leverage can increase the rate of return substantially, even by several folds.

When my wife and I first started to buy townhouses as rental properties, both our real estate agent and loan officer told us that the regulation was that we could only obtain a maximum of four loans. I called several loan officers and the answer was the same. But I kept checking around and one day, a loan officer said that he found a bank that would allow a maximum of ten loans to qualified borrowers. That enabled us to buy more townhouses.

Eventually we maxed out with ten loans, including eight mortgages on townhouses, a mortgage on our primary residence, and a HELOC (home equity line of credit) which we took out from our primary home to help pay for another townhouse.

Because these rental properties were spitting out cash every month, we were accumulating cash at a faster rate that we otherwise could with only our salaries. While being unable to obtain more loans, with the cash accumulation, we eventually bought two townhouses with cash in the span of about four years.

An advantage of buying with a cash offer is that we can tell the seller that we are serious buyers and we can close quickly. Then we offer a price that is below the market.

Some sellers have had prospective buyers who failed to get a loan, and who walked away. Therefore, a cash offer has appeal to the sellers and they are willing to accept a slightly lower price in exchange for the certainty.

After buying two townhouses with cash, we had exhausted our cash. In fact, for one of the townhouses, we had to borrow money from our 401k accounts in order to close the deal. My wife and I had each borrowed about $50,000 from our 401k accounts, and as long as we paid back in the designated time period, there was no penalty. We closed the deal on the townhouse, and then used the cash-flow from the rental properties to pay back the 401k loans quickly. Not everyone should be borrowing from their 401k accounts, but if you urgently need cash to save a good deal, and if the property will yield significant cash-flow, then 401k could be another borrowing source to consider. Just make sure that you consult with your tax accountant and pay back the 401k loan quickly.

One day in 2015, I had a handyman come around to fix some of our windows. I told him that I had been investing in residential real estate, and hoped to expand into commercial real estate, and needed a mentor. The handyman kindly told me that he had worked for a gentleman who did well in real estate, and that he would connect the two of us.

This gentleman was LK, who later sold us his office condo in 2017. LK was friendly and kind, and willing to teach. In early 2017, when he heard that we had maxed out on loans, he generously offered to give us a personal loan of $500,000, using the two townhouses that we had paid in cash as collateral. We met his lawyer and signed the paperwork for the loan, and we had more money to buy more properties.

After we settled on the LK office condo, I kept in touch with the loan officers in that local commercial bank that we used (let's refer to this commercial bank as A). The loan officers were friendly. They got to know our situation well and understood the cash-flow that we were having.

By then, we had purchased two more townhouses without mortgages, and commercial bank A was able to get us approved for a commercial line of credit (LOC) for $500,000, using those two townhouses free of mortgages as collateral. A commercial LOC is useful because if we do not borrow any money from it, we do not need to pay any interest. When we find a good deal, we can take money out of the LOC to make the purchase, then use the cash-flow to pay back the LOC, thus making the LOC available for the next purchase.

If we had not opened the commercial LOC, our alternative method would be to do a cash-out refinance on the two townhouses that did not have mortgages. It is a good method and we have used it in other occasions. However, a small disadvantage of cash-out refinance is that, right after the settlement, we would need to start to pay interest on the cashed-out amount every month. If we find a good deal to invest this cash, that would be great. But if we were unable to find a good deal to purchase, then we would be paying interest on the cashed-out amount for nothing.

After we had settled on our office building, I got connected with the other commercial bank that gave us the loan for the office building (let's refer to this local commercial bank as B). In the early spring of 2019, I found a short-sale townhouse. I made a cash offer that was abut 10% below the market, and got the deal.

We took money out of the commercial LOC to pay cash for this townhouse. We made repairs and rented out the townhouse. Then bank B approved a cash-out refinance on this townhouse. We used the cash-out money to pay back the bulk of the loan from the commercial LOC. We did this for two reasons. (1) The cash-out refinance on this townhouse can lock in the interest rate for a relatively long time (7 years in this case), while the commercial LOC rate is floating; and (2) By using the cash-out money to pay back the bulk of the LOC, we make the LOC available for another purchase if we find a good deal in the future.

Therefore, to expand in real estate investing and to achieve a good rates of return, it is critically important to make use of good leverages and loans. To raise the necessary funding, it pays to keep trying and not give up, to talk to loan officers and banks, and to be decent and responsible and trustworthy so that others are willing to trust you and help you.

Furthermore, as you accumulate more properties that produce cash every month, the cash-flow will be counted as part of your income by the lender, thus further enabling you to qualify for more loans.

Moreover, when you gradually pay down the principal in the properties, plus price appreciation after several years, you will have sizable equity in the properties. This will enable you to do cash-out refinances to have more funds to buy more properties. These additional properties will produce even more cash, and put you into a virtuous cycle.

In addition, it helps to have friends who trust you enough to be your partners to invest with you, as with our LK property and the office building. One thing will lead to another, and you will eventually achieve things that you could not have imagined when you first started out.

This chapter focuses on funds. Once you have some funds, how to get started in screening for the suitable rental properties? How to negotiate and get the best possible deal? These will be the focus of the next chapter.

Chapter 10. The What, When, and How in Buying Rental Properties

I had seen high yield bonds when the market priced them like flowers and I had seen them when they were considered weeds. I liked them better when they were weeds.

-- Warren Buffett

After eight years of investing in rental properties, I have learned some valuable lessons about what would qualify as being a good rental property, what time in the year would usually be the best time to get the best possible deals, and how to purchase a property at a relatively low price. Some of my methods were developed after making mistakes. Some of the lessons were learned after paying a price. The purpose of this chapter is to help you get started to buy the right types of rental properties and know how to negotiate to get your offer accepted by the seller, while paying the lowest possible price.

What types of properties to buy. There are many good ways to invest in real estate. Some people like to buy old and deteriorated properties, make major renovations, then either sell for a quick profit (flip), or rent out for the long-term (hold). With a full-time job and limited time to spend on real estate, I prefer to buy structurally-sound and relatively new townhouses near good schools. Preferably, the house is dirty and has many minor damages, such as dirty carpet, dirty walls, holes in walls, cracks in doors, fractured windows, etc. These things turn off many buyers, reducing the competition. But these things are relatively easy and inexpensive to fix, and I can likely get a good deal on the house. For example, in 2012, the house BD had a lot of damage in the basement and we bought it for $241,000 and spent $11,000 to fix it, for a total of $252,000. But the fair market value then was $275,000 to $285,000. Hence, we saved about 10%.

In our recent purchase, the townhouse had dirty carpet, dirty walls, and a leaky roof. The townhouse was 17 years old, still not too old. It is in my neighborhood and I know the area and these houses well. We made a cash offer at $285,000, which was accepted. We spent about $10,000 to fix everything. So, our total cost was about $295,000. Similar houses in the same neighborhood were selling at $330,000 to $340,000. We then did a cash-out refinance, and the lender approved our request to pull out $249,000. This left only $46,000 of our own money in this house. As shown in previous chapters, reducing our own money in the house increases the rate of return on the invested capital.

When we first started to buy rental townhouses, there were a few houses that we walked away from that I later regretted. I will share them here, so that you will not miss the good opportunities and then later feel the same regret.

For example, one townhouse had dirty floors, fist holes in the walls, kicking fractures in bedroom doors, and ketchup stains on the cabinet and on the ceiling of the kitchen. There were rumors that the sellers were losing the house to the bank and were struggling, and they probably had some angry fights that caused this damage.

I told my agent that I wanted to make an offer of $242,000, and I discussed with my wife, but we did not submit the offer during a moment of hesitation. The house was later sold to another buyer for $240,000, as public record later showed. The market value for that house at that time was $275,000 - $285,000. The house was only 6 years old at that time, and it had a huge backyard with excellent open views.

These and similar houses are the "trouble" houses that many buyers walk away from, but are actually the ones that you should look for and focus on. Only after I lost it did I realize how good and rare of an opportunity that was. I kept looking and have not found a similarly good deal. Once an opportunity is gone, it's gone.

An experienced investor recognizes a good deal when he/she sees one. Without the knowledge, training and experience, opportunities can be screaming in the faces of people and they still don't see it. Houses like these have excellent rates of return. Therefore, it pays to focus on the numbers, not merely the appearances.

When to purchase. If you look hard enough, good deals can be found year-round. Personally, I prefer to look during bitter cold winters, preferably with thick snow and ice on the ground. My experience in the past eight years in my area is that there are better deals in the winter, and there are fewer buyers, if any, competing for the houses.

Some of the houses that were still on the market in the winter started to be on the market in the spring. They did not close successfully in the spring, summer, and fall. Therefore, by the time it is winter, the sellers may have become softened, are more flexible, and are even a little desperate.

In the frozen winter, few buyers are looking for houses. Then I make a cash offer. I waive the financial contingency because I do not need a loan. I waive the inspection contingency because I buy only relatively new houses in the neighborhood that I know well. These approaches sometimes help me get a good deal that is 5-10% below the market. If the house is in a cosmetically poor condition, it is possible to get even a little more than 5-10% below the market. However, I do not recommend that you waive the inspection contingency if you are buying older houses or if there is reason to suspect the structural soundness.

These cash offers in the cold of winter have a good likelihood of being accepted, because the seller sees that the buyer is serious, has waived some contingencies, and can close quickly. Then after the settlement, we can do a cash-out refinance to pull out the bulk of the cash to increase the rate of return, and also to be ready to purchase the next deal.

Another good method is to open a home equity line of credit (HELOC), and use the HELOC to buy a house or two in the winter. Then you can use the cash-flow from all your properties to pay back the HELOC in the following months. Then winter comes again and you repeat this method. Additionally, because the properties that you purchased with cash from the HELOC have no mortgages, you may do a cash-out refinance to pull cash out to pay back the HELOC.

How to get a good deal. The goal is to buy a property by offering the lowest possible price while still being able to close the deal. The price you pay determines your profit, cash-flow, and whether you succeed or not. Provide things that the seller needs and values. For example, most buyers need to apply for a loan to buy the house; some buyers may submit a contract to buy, but then walk away later, citing the reason of loan difficulty and financial contingency.

In addition, some sellers worry that the buyers may change their mind and walk away after an inspection finding small issues. Therefore, if you make a cash offer and waive some contingencies, you provide certainty to the seller. In return, you may get the house even if your offer is lower.

Here are some ways that you can make a cash offer:

(1) You can accumulate cash from your salary income, but depending on your income level, this may take some time.

(2) If you have significant equity in your primary residence, you can open a HELOC to make a cash offer on your next property. The advantage is that you can take the money out of the HELOC only when you are ready to settle on a rental property. If you do not find a good rental property to buy and do not take money out of the HELOC, you pay no interest. After settlement on the rental property, then you do a cash-out refinance to pull the bulk of your money out of the new property. You use that money to pay back the HELOC, making it available for your next purchase.

(3). After several years, if you have substantial equity in some of your rental properties, you may do a cash-out refinance to pull the cash out. This not only increases the rate of return on the existing rental property, but also provides you the ability to make a cash offer to buy your next property.

(4). Form an LLC and obtain a commercial LOC using your rental properties as collateral. Borrow money from the LOC to make a cash offer to purchase a new rental property. Then do a cash-out refinance on the rental property to pay back the bulk of the LOC, and use the cash-flow from your rentals to pay back the rest of the LOC. Then you can use the LOC again to buy the next property. Then repeat.

Besides making cash offers, there are other ways to pay a lower price to buy a house. I have had sellers ask if we would allow them to leave some junk behind in the house when they move out, such as old sofas, and old and huge TV sets. While most buyers would say no, I have always said yes. This makes me and my offer stand out to the seller, and makes it more likely for the seller to accept my offer. If I could save $5,000 on the purchase, and then pay someone $500 to remove the junk, why not?

In addition, I have used another method to help obtain good deals. I have asked my real estate agent to copy and paste the following message and email it to the seller's agent:

"We are serious buyers and would very much like to close this deal. We do not plan to walk away and would like to go all the way to the settlement table, so that the agents will get paid."

The real estate agents rely on commissions as their incomes, and they appreciate messages like this. They appreciate a serious and committed buyer. This message will encourage the agent to try to convince the seller to accept our offer although it may be a little low, rather than accepting another higher offer from a buyer who may walk away in the process before settlement. Other buyers may have various uncertainties, which may cause the deal to fall through.

Getting a good deal and paying less for the house has significant benefits. It cannot be over-emphasized that paying less for the house has double benefits:

(1) Paying less for the house increases your rate of return for that house.

(2) Even more importantly, by leaving less money in each house, you will accumulate money faster and buy the next property more quickly, thereby accumulating more properties.

Let's use our recent purchase of a townhouse as an example. We paid $285,000 in cash and spent $10,000 for repairs (totaling $295,000), for a house that was worth $330,000 to $340,000. We then did a cash-out refinance and pulled out $249,000 cash. Therefore, we had $46,000 of our own money in this house.

Now let's say that you are able to repeat this method to do the exact same deals. For every house that you buy, you sink $46,000 of your own money into the house, and the rest is the lender's money.

Therefore, in order to buy a rental house, you need to save $46,000 cash. Let's call this case A.

Now let's compare with case B. In case B, in contrast, let's say that instead of paying $295,000 for that townhouse, you paid $340,000 (the full market price) to buy that townhouse.

Then you do a cash-out refinance. The lender allows you to pull 75% cash out: $340,000 x 75% = $255,000. Now the amount of your own money invested in this house is: $340,000 - $255,000 = $85,000.

The important point is: It will take you much longer to save $85,000 than to save only $46,000.

Of course, in both A and B, you will also need to save some extra money to pay for closing costs, but that part would be similar in both cases A and B.

This comparison clearly demonstrates that paying more for the house (case B) will slow you down and reduce the number of houses that you can purchase in the same given period of time (say, 10 years), compared to case A.

Therefore, you should strive to pay less when you purchase a house, by diligently looking and screening for good deals; using good negotiation techniques described in this chapter such as providing what the seller needs and making cash offers; and buying a house in a cosmetically poor condition - the poorer, the better.

In this way, you will not only achieve a higher rate of return on each house, but also, more importantly, accumulate many more real estate properties at a quicker speed.

After you have acquired several properties, you may feel busy, tired, and even overwhelming, dealing with paperwork, tenants, repairs, etc. The nervousness about what unpleasant things may happen in the future adds to the emotional stress. I still remember that one night, I woke up in the middle of the night and felt so overwhelmed when I had accumulated five rental houses. Having to manage five rental houses put a lot of emotional stress on me. I started to reach out for help and to have a team to support me. You will need a team to support you, which is the focus of the next chapter.

Chapter 11. Building a Team

Great things in business are never done by one person. They're done by a team of people.

-- Steve Jobs

You may be getting excited to start investing in real estate, but have concerns that you have a full-time job. It is prudent that you keep your job and do not quit your job too early, until your real estate cash-flow has enabled you to achieve financial freedom. Can you do real estate investing on the side, while being a full-time employee?

The answer is yes, if you build and rely on a team. I devote 50+ hours per week to my job. And I have three kids. Therefore, I cannot afford to spend much time on real estate investing. If you also have a busy job and think that you have no time to invest in real estate, I hope that this chapter will inspire you and help open your eyes to the possibilities.

By using a good team, I generally spend only several hours a month on real estate investing (perhaps 2-3 hours per week, or around 10 hours per month on average). I am pretty sure that you can save 10 hours in a month by watching a little less TV, and spending a little less time on the internet and the smart phone. Ten some hours per month is only about half an hour per day in average.

It is critically important to build a team to help you invest in real estate. Even if you want to invest in real estate full-time, you will still need a good team. Whether you do it full-time, or keep your day job and spend only a few hours weekly on real estate investing, you should learn to use other people's time and other people's talents. You will need a network of friends, mentor(s), real estate agents, loan officers, handymen, various contractors, etc.

In this chapter, instead of detailing a laundry list of what team members that you will need, I will share my experience and knowledge of how to gradually build a team. Do not let "I don't have a team" to be an excuse to stop you from getting started to invest in real estate. It's OK if you do not have a team. Most of us do not have a team when we first start out. I did not have a team in the first few years of real estate investing. In addition, I will also describe how to treat your team members well, and respect them and their time. This will help you to recruit and retain the excellent team members.

Build your team one member at a time, gradually, along your real estate investing journey. When I first started out, I had no idea that I would need someone to walk on the roof. In the process of buying our second townhouse, there was a leak in a bedroom ceiling, and my real estate agent called a guy who went onto the roof and sealed the leak. That instance made me realize how it was important to have a guy like that. I kept in touch with him and relied on him for several years to perform roof repairs, clean the gutters, and even trim the trees. Then he got older and did not want to climb the roofs anymore, so my handyman researched and found another roof person, and he has been doing an excellent job with my rental properties for the past several years.

Therefore, do not worry if you do not have a team to start with. It is more important to actually get started on investing in real estate. Then along the way, take the time to gradually build up your team, one member at a time.

Some of the lessons were learned in a hurry. On a hot summer day, a tenant reported that the central AC system was not working, and that the house temperature was at 90 degrees. We had to find an AC repair person quickly. One contractor came and replaced the AC system. However, he did not replace the furnace that was connected with the AC and used for heating in the winter. The following winter, we found that the furnace also needed to be replaced. So, he came back again and replaced the furnace. For this specific type of HVAC (heating, ventilation, and air conditioning) system, replacing the AC and furnace separately almost doubled the labor cost because one was on the top of the other and had to be dissembled. It cost me a bit more than $1,000 extra, which I did not realize at that time.

Later, we bought another townhouse where we replaced the HVAC system. The first HVAC contractor was out of town, so I found another contractor to do it, and his total charge for both the AC and the heating system was about $1,000 less than the first person. These were similar townhouses with similar HVAC systems. He explained to me that for these townhouses, it is more cost-effective to replace the AC and heating system at the same time.

After that, I stopped using the first guy and continued to use the second guy for several years. He was very good and responsible, but had another day job and could only come in the evenings and on the weekends, so he was not always fast. Eventually, I found a third HVAC expert who does a very good and efficient job. He is a top-notch expert and charges reasonable prices. I have been using him exclusively ever since.

The moral of this experience is:

(1) Do not worry if you don't have a team at the start. Don't let the lack of a team stop you from starting to invest in real estate. You will build your team, one member at a time, along your real estate journey.

(2) You may have to go through a few candidates before you finally find a really good team member. So, keep searching and be open-minded.

(3) It is OK to make mistakes along the way. This is the normal learning and growing process.

Be faithful and responsible to your team members.
This one might seem obvious but can be easy to forget in the heat of the moment when you are chasing a good deal or need a problem fixed. As I mentioned earlier, for the townhouse PS, the seller's agent was playing tricks in an attempt to keep the whole commission to himself and not pay my agent. We were eventually able to buy the house with cash by selling our 529 funds. Part of my driving force was to get this townhouse, but the other part was that I wanted my agent to get paid to reward her for her time and effort. It is important to get your agent paid to keep her as a good member of your team.

In another instance, we were at the settlement table to buy another townhouse, and the settlement company added about a $300 additional fee in the HUD-1 for us, the buyer, to pay. My agent was arguing with the settlement lawyer that this fee was not reasonable and should be removed. The settlement lawyer agreed that this fee was questionable, but it was a late afternoon on a Friday and he would need to consult with his boss the next Monday. However, there was no guarantee that his boss would agree; plus, we would need to come back again next Tuesday to complete the settlement.

At this point, I said that I appreciated my agent's effort to save us money, but I did not want to waste her and others' time. Spending several more hours next week would not be worth it, and I wanted her to receive her commission payment today. So, my wife and I paid the extra $300 and finished the settlement, and everybody went home happy. These small things will gradually add up and help win you a good team member.

Value their time and honor their efforts. I have a wonderful handyman LW. He is intelligent, capable, faithful and loyal. He always makes the extra effort. Those are the types of people that it can be easy to take for granted. LW told me that once another homeowner asked LW to replace some flooring. LW went to the individual's house, took the measurements, and discussed options for the type and style of flooring with the homeowner. The next day, LW went to Home Depot, bought the materials, and hauled everything to the homeowner's house, ready to work. To his surprise, the homeowner told LW that he had changed his mind and did not need his work anymore. Disappointed, LW drove back to Home Depot and returned the materials. He did not argue with that guy, but he never worked with for again. The homeowner wasted LW's time and as a result, lost a valuable team member.

Whenever LW does something for me, I do not hide my respect and appreciation. I text him and shower him with sincere praises: "Thank you so much!" "You are the best!" I give him tips. I send him presents on holidays. The best handymen do not lack work. They are busy. Like us, they would rather work for someone who appreciates them.

Appreciation and respect will help them to do an even better job for you.

Tipping them well. I once hired a carpenter handyman to install some windows in my house. I treated him well and gave him a nice tip. During our conversation, I mentioned that I'd love to find a mentor on real estate investing. He kindly introduced me to LK. This led to a good friendship, the acquisition of the LK office condo, which in turn led to the purchase of the office building.

Granted, this does not happen every time you give a tip. However, it is beneficial to be kind to others, and to treat others with respect and generosity. By doing so, you will be doing the right thing and creating win-win situations.

As another example, for my HVAC repairs, I give the repair person a tip of $50, sometimes $100. They take my calls and come as soon as possible. ACs usually break in hot weather when they are needed the most, and AC repair people are the busiest during these seasons because many other ACs also tend to break in the same hot weather. It is important to have a good AC repair person on your team whom you treat well, and who can come quickly to your rental properties. The same can be said for heating systems in cold winters.

Recommend them to others and bring them more businesses. I have used a real estate lawyer on several occasions. He is expensive, but does a good job. Whenever I have an opportunity, I recommend him to other landlords. For example, one day, a friend who is a medical doctor in another state contacted me. He had some rental properties in my state and needed a lawyer. I recommended my lawyer to him and connected them through email. In addition, if I ever hear that someone plans to buy a house and needs a real estate agent, I recommend my agent. Help your team members and make an effort to bring more opportunities to them. Do what you can through networking and recommendations to help them be successful.

These constructive actions will help build up your team. They will help you expand your real estate investments far beyond what you can achieve by yourself single-handedly. This will enable you to make the best use of other people's time and other people's talents. Then you can focus on growing your real estate investment without being burned out and without carrying a lot of emotional stress, which is the focus of the next chapter.

Chapter 12. Other People's Time and My Emotional Detachment

When I was a kid, there was no collaboration; it's you with a camera bossing your friends around. But as an adult, filmmaking is all about appreciating the talents of the people you surround yourself with and knowing you could never have made any of these films by yourself.

-- Steven Spielberg, Hollywood filmmaker

Once you have a team, humbly manage, diligently delegate, and respectfully use other people's talents and time. Time management is all about delegation. I routinely spend 50+ hours per week on my job. On some days, I may spend a few hours to take care of real estate matters; on many other days, I spend no time at all on real estate. I do not play golf. I watch only half an hour of news daily. The three hours per week that others would spend watching TV or searching the internet, I spent on real estate.

As a productive scientist, I have made sure that my job has a high priority, and my real estate investing does not negatively affect my job.

If you learn how to respect and use other people's time, it is certainly feasible to invest in real estate on the side, while still maintaining excellent performance at your full-time job. I have three kids, and I am not strong physically and emotionally. I am not one of those people who need only 4-6 hours of sleep; I need 8 hours of sleep. Therefore, if I can invest in real estate on the side, so can you.

The beauty of real estate investing is that you can use other people's money, other people's time, and other people's talents. In the following sections, I will describe the process of buying a house and renting it out to tenants, and how other people's time is used in the entire process.

My agent regularly emails me a link with townhouses for sale in my "farm" area, which is my neighborhood. If I see a townhouse that has the potential to be a good deal, I ask my handyman to walk through the house with me, which takes about 10-15 minutes.

All the townhouses that I have bought are within walking distance from where I live. The reason is time and experience. I have lived here for 16 years. I know the area and the houses very well, and it takes only a short time to check out a house.

In contrast, if I wanted to buy a house that was 30 minutes or an hour away from where I live, I would need to spend much more time to research and investigate to get more information. Furthermore, the other investor buyer who lives near that house would have a competitive edge over me.

Therefore, I have only focused on my own neighborhood. It has about three thousand houses, hence there are plenty of houses to buy for a small investor like me. If you are a small investor like me, I strongly suggest that you focus on your own neighborhood, and limit your purchases to within a few miles from where you live.

The more familiar you are with the location and the houses, (1) the less the time that you have to spend to investigate, (2) the less the risk that you are taking, (3) the more the confidence and conviction that you will have, and therefore, (4) the more likely that you will succeed in closing the deal.

In contrast, if you are not so sure and confident about a deal, you may waiver during the negotiations and walk away. There will be plenty of opportunities for you in your own neighborhood. That is where you can become an expert, and that is where you will have a competitive edge.

During those 10-15 minutes of walk-through, my handyman would tell me what needs to be fixed and how much the approximate cost will be. My handyman is very talented. I do not have his talents. With his help, I can determine how much money is needed, and what my offer price and negotiation range should be in order to get a good deal. Then I email my real estate agent to ask her to submit my offer. If we do successfully get this deal, then after the settlement, I give the keys to my handyman and he does the necessary repairs, etc. In addition, if in the rare case that the roof needs work, I call a roofer. If the carpet needs to be replaced, I call a carpet contractor. If the HVAC needs replacing, I call my HVAC contractor. These items take only 5 minutes here and 5 minutes there.

Once the house is in move-in condition, I ask my real estate agent to put it on the market and to show it to prospective tenants. She finds the tenant and prepares the lease to be signed. Nowadays, she has us sign the lease electronically through email, which saves even more time. The bank routing number and account numbers are provided to the tenants for them to pay the security deposit and rent. If the tenants have further repair needs in the house after they move in, I ask them to contact my handyman and contractors directly; it is easier for them to directly make an appointment that is good for both sides than for me to be the middleman.

As you can see, this whole process takes only a few hours of my time. Of course, as you gain more experience in real estate investing, you may figure out other ways to save even more time and increase the efficiency of your process.

After owning a few rental properties and gradually building up your team, you will have a network and a list of various experts and contractors. Once you have established a good working relationship with them, then what you do will be just some emails, texts and phone calls, when the need arises.

If you have a full-time job, you can further reduce the need for your time on real estate matters if you buy structurally sound and relatively new houses, thereby reducing the need for repairs.

Another benefit of using other people's time and talents is that it helps me to stay emotionally detached. I am a light sleeper; this strategy of using other people's time and talents has helped me to sleep better. I have found that if I get into too much detail in real estate, my mind will become clogged and burdened, and this has negative effects on me emotionally.

By using other people's time and talents as much as possible, I can focus on buying, funding, strategy and bigger picture items. I can maintain a clear head, and not let the details clog my mind.

I know my weaknesses. I am a relatively weak person physically and emotionally. Frankly, if I had to do many of the details and some of the repair and maintenance work by myself, if I had to focus on the dirt and the damage in the house, I would have been burned out. I would have lost my enthusiasm and would have had no interest to buy more properties, and we would have ended up with much fewer assets, less wealth and less cash-flow.

Yes, you have to pay your team members and pay them well. However, thanks to using their time and talents, you can expand to, say, 14 properties, instead of, say, only 5 houses. Owning 14 cash-producing properties will grow your wealth much faster than 5 properties.

Therefore, paying for other people's time is not a negative factor on your wealth. On the contrary, it will enable you to expand your real estate investing and accumulate rental properties faster. The money that you spend on paying for other people's time will more than pay for itself.

In my experience, paying for other people's time has helped me to reduce stress, focus on bigger picture issues, and acquire more properties. Paying for other people's time will free up your mind to think and find bigger and better opportunities, which will be the focus of the next chapter.

Chapter 13. Train Your Eyes to See Opportunities

Without training and preparation, opportunity can scream in people's faces and they won't see it.

--Unknown

Using a good team will free you from many of the time-consuming details, and enable you to have a clear head to focus on the big picture issues. Your big picture is: to gradually and safely expand your real estate empire, find opportunities, raise funds, avoid pitfalls, increase cash-flow, and achieve your financial freedom. These topics are the focus of the current and the following chapters.

The ability to see the finished fine product through the dirt and rubble. In the 1990s, my mentor LK saw a dilapidated factory building. The building had been deserted for years. He then went on vacation with his wife in Europe for a month.

When he returned, there was still no buyer for that building. While others saw an old factory building with broken or missing windows and the basement under water, he saw that this building was in a good location in the city and was structurally sound. So, he went to the city and offered to buy the eyesore, renovate it into an office building, and rent the space out to companies. The city liked his idea of not only removing a headache for them, but also attracting companies to move in and creating jobs. LK bought this building and the associated land for pennies on the dollar.

LK's experienced eyes saw four main things:

(1) Through the debris, dust, broken pieces and the pond in the basement, he saw that the structure of the building, including the foundation, walls and floors, were in good condition.

(2) Instead of turning it into a modern-style building which would have been much more expensive to do, he saw the opportunity to turn it into an antique-looking building with the feel of a museum. He collected old artifacts and historic photos, and displayed them throughout this building to tell the story of the history of this neighborhood. He knew that there were companies and employees who would enjoy working in an environment rich in history and heritage.

(3) He refurbished the main building, which was about 33,000 square feet. He decided to tear down a couple of separate and small structures on this land to develop a large parking lot with over 100 parking spaces. He saw that in the busy downtown area, having enough surface parking spaces right next to the building would greatly increase the appeal of this office building.

(4) After finishing this antique-looking and museum-like office building, he set up a condo structure and sold the seven condos one by one to various buyers. He saw that it was easier to sell individual units than to sell the entire building. These units were purchased either by companies for their own use, or by investors who rented them out to tenant companies.

Because his trained eyes saw the right things to do, this building has attracted the attention of many companies and has seen nearly 100% occupancy during most of its past 20+ years.

LK made a profit of about $7 million on this building alone, from rents and sales proceeds. Meanwhile, he did a valuable service to the city and the community by turning around and reviving this neighborhood. His wealth has enabled him to give generously to charities. Therefore, what is wealth? Trained and experienced eyes are wealth. What is a money tree? Trained and experienced eyes are money trees.

The ability to see the future trend. As people say: "The trend is your friend". Every time I visit China which I do about once a year, I would have lunch or dinner with my friend Rong. After the former Chinese leader, Mr. Deng Xiaoping, opened its door to the world, China has made amazing progress and its economy has boomed in the past three decades. This made China the second largest economy in the world behind the U.S. Since the 1990s, my friend Rong has been an entrepreneur in the textile business, starting small and gradually growing his factory. About a decade ago, through hard work and with help of the flourishing Chinese economy, he had accumulated about 10 million yuan (the exchange ratio was about $1 to 7 yuan), which was certainly admirable and worthy of celebration.

However, at that time which was a decade ago, Rong saw a worrisome future trend. His textile factory used relatively inexpensive machines and average-level technology, which was a relatively low threshold to enter. The success and the low threshold had attracted a lot of other entrepreneurs to this industry.

He saw the possibility that the competition would kill profits, the supply would exceed the demand, and many of these entrepreneurs would fold in the not-so-distant future.

Rong looked at his 10 million yuan, and he faced a choice: (1) Keep this 10 million in the bank for his and his family's future, and continue the status quo. If in case the factory has to close in the future, he and his family would have enough to live on. (2) Use this 10 million to upgrade his factory by purchasing advanced, high-quality machinery. In other words, take a risk to try to increase quality and capability to a level that would be hard to compete with. However, if he failed in this major shift, then his 10 million fortune would be gone.

Rong told me that he contemplated this big move for days, without discussing with anyone, for fear that others' opinions would cloud his sharp focus on the future trend. One night, he kept thinking about this and did not sleep. He said: "The next morning, I got up, clenched my teeth, and threw that 10 million yuan into my factory."

This bold and savvy move saved his factory from faltering like many others did years later. It took him a couple of years to implement the upgrade in new equipment and new product lines. The result is: In the past seven years, his factory has been spitting out about 10 million yuan profit every year. In 2018, even during the trade war, he made 15 million yuan in profit, largely due to his great efficiency in making high-quality and advanced textiles that other factories simply cannot replicate.

Rise above the noise and focus on the numbers. On a smaller scale that may be more feasible for small investors like me, I saw a townhouse damaged by fire that was near one of my rental properties. My real estate agent told me that the owner failed to pay the mortgage, hence the house was entering into the short-sale process; the owner wanted to defraud the insurance company and set the house on fire. He was planning to claim that the fire was an accident, to get paid from the insurance company for the damages, and then take the money and leave. I did not follow the story and am not sure how that claim went or if there was an investigation. The neighbors saw the fire and called 911. By the time the fire was put out, it had burned a hole in the second floor and roof, damaged the back wall, and burned the deck in the backyard.

I went to look at this house twice, first by myself and my agent, and then with some friends. I wanted to make an offer in the range of $200k to $220k, estimating that it would take about $60k to $70k to restore the house to move-in condition.

However, everyone I talked to was against it. They reasoned that the damage looked terrible, and it looked like too much work and too much trouble. So, I did not proceed.

Several months later, I happened to pass by and saw that this townhouse had been completely renovated and was on the market for sale. I saw someone who was moving some stuff into that townhouse. I talked with him, and he said that he was an investor who flipped houses. He had bought this house for $200k, and had put in about $50k for renovations. After a few weeks, the house was sold for $335k, turning him a nice profit. If he could flip three to four houses like this every year, that would be a very good income.

If I had bought that house, I would have kept it as a rental property. As demonstrated in previous chapters, I could do a cash-out refinance later on. If I could buy a $335k house with only $260k (purchase price + repair costs etc.), and then pull out, say, 75% of the appraisal value of $335k (75% x $335,000 = $251,250), I would leave only a small amount of my own money in the house. This in turn would yield an excellent rate of return on the invested capital.

Whether sell it or keep it as a rental property, this was a very good deal. This was a good opportunity that I had missed, against my better judgment.

Therefore, if you want to be a good investor, it is important to rise above the noise and focus on the numbers to avoid missing good opportunities.

Furthermore, to look for and be able to see the opportunities, it is important to expand your mind to think bigger. A narrow mind will limit you and cause you to miss the opportunities. Thinking big will enable you to see more and greater opportunities. This will be the focus of the next chapter.

Chapter 14. Think Big

I like thinking big. I always have. To me it's very simple: if you are going to be thinking anyway, you might as well think big.

--Donald J. Trump

In 2010, I thought that I was thinking big when I told my real estate agent that I would like to buy five houses as rental properties. Now that my wife and I have acquired 14 rental properties, I was apparently not thinking big enough then. Indeed, there are others who think much bigger.

From small to big. The book "Rich Dad Poor Dad" is a well-known best-seller on personal financial education. Its author Mr. Robert Kiyosaki has helped improve the personal financial literacy of millions of people. In his other book, "Unfair Advantage: The Power of Financial Education", he recalled his humble beginning, when he bought his first rental property in 1973, pocketing a meager $25 cash-flow per month, after paying the mortgage and other expenses (page 223 in "Unfair Advantage").

Since then, he and his wife Kim have continued to invest and gradually grown their investing empire. In 2012, they bought $87 million worth of real estate in one year alone (page 224 in "Unfair Advantage").

In addition, after becoming a popular author of personal financial books, Mr. Kiyosaki was invited by Mr. Donald Trump to team up to write financial books. The two of them published books together, including "Why We Want You To Be Rich: Two Men One Message," which was published in 2006.

Mr. Kiyosaki's books have been translated into more than fifty languages and are available in more than a hundred countries. For someone who almost failed high school, it took "thinking big" to become a best-selling author who has influenced so many people around the world. It took "thinking big" to come up with creative ideas and financial strategies to put deals together and take risks to acquire $87 million of real estate properties in a single year. It took "thinking big" to overcome the fear and nervousness to ascend to the national and international stages, and to be featured on famous shows such as "Larry King Live" and "Oprah".

From nobody to a household name. A year ago, my son, then a junior in a university majoring in business, told me: "Dad, there is an Asian guy running for president, his name is Andrew Yang, and I am going to vote for him."

I said: "Really? He is an unknown. Why do you want to vote for him?"

My son is a top-of-the-class straight A student (and he recently graduated with the honor of Summa Cum Laude). He answered me: "At first I thought Yang's proposals were ridiculous. Then I spent hours researching and studying and listening. And I realized that he actually had deeper justifications to benefit the country that made sense."

Since then, I have paid attention to Mr. Andrew Yang, his message, reasoning, and explanations. He has clearly pointed out the mega-trend risk of mass job losses due to automation, and how this country can prepare for a better future by empowering the people. You may agree with his policy proposals, or you may not. That's not the point here.

The point here is: he went from an unknown person to a household name throughout the entire country, and he has demonstrated his excellent analytical skills and his clear big-picture ideas. While I cannot predict the future, this will likely open the door to vast opportunities for him in the future. It certainly is possible that someday he could be appointed as the secretary of a department or a cabinet member in a future White House administration, or that he could choose to run to become a senator or a congressman. In addition, he could write books. Companies and organizations and universities would invite him to give speeches. These opportunities would have been unimaginable if he were not thinking big.

Therefore, thinking big can open the doors to otherwise unimaginable opportunities, can lead to new horizons, can produce enormous benefits, and can change the trajectory of your life and the lives of others.

Ignore the nay-sayers and listen to experts who have actually done it. Thinking big and putting it into action will cause you to come across difficulties, challenges, doubts and nay-sayers. I have a good friend in China, Wu, and we would meet for lunch or dinner when I visit relatives in China. In the 1990s, he saw a muddy rice field for sale. He visited the city's development office and saw the city's plan to expand in that direction in the future, which would mean that more people would move there and new stores would open there.

He wanted to buy this land, but he did not have enough money. So, he talked with several people to try to convince them to pool money together to buy this land, and then apply for loans to develop it. They visited the site and listened to his description of future plans, but did not want to take the risk. So instead, he found a bank that was willing to give him a loan to buy this land, using this land as collateral, after he agreed to pour all of his savings into it as down payment.

He acquired this land and slowly developed some residential condos. He sold the condos and used the cash as down payment to get more loans to develop more buildings.

Wu eventually built several five-story buildings on that land, with the top four levels as residential condo units, and the ground level as stores.

A couple of years ago, when we met again and had dinner together, he estimated that he made about 90 million yuan in that deal. He said that he had to overcome the self-doubts and the doubting words of nay-sayers. He told me that he followed the book "Rick Dad Poor Dad" which he had read multiple times, and it served as his light in the darkness. Where others saw only a muddy land, he saw a future vision of grand new buildings. He was thinking big, and as a result, was handsomely rewarded.

However, to think big is one thing; to actually pull the trigger, take the risk and take the plunge is another. This will be the focus of the next chapter.

Chapter 15. Pull the Trigger, Take the Risk, and Manage the Risk

I knew from being a poker player that you have to bet heavily when you've got huge odds in your favor.
-- Charles Munger, Vice Chairman of Berkshire Hathaway, Buffett's partner

Now that you have reached this chapter, you already know my humble real-life examples, how to get started as a novice investor, the useful methods, the lucrative approaches, and the important essentials to begin in real estate investing.

However, my experience is that it may still be difficult for someone who has not invested in real estate before to actually pull the trigger. You may be aiming and aiming, but just can't muster enough courage to pull the trigger. This is a phenomenon called analysis paralysis, which a lot of people have. So, this chapter is written for you.

Several years ago, while visiting China, I had dinner with an entrepreneur and owner of a construction cement factory. After a couple of glasses of wine, I asked him: "If you look back at your entrepreneurial journey, what is the single most important factor that has led to your success today?"

He thought for a moment and told me this story:

"In the 1990s, I was working in a government-owned construction cement factory, and the government wanted to sell this factory and get it privatized. The price was 500,000 yuan. That was a ton of money back then. That was much more than all the money I had. I told my wife that I wanted to buy the factory, improve it and expand the business. But if I failed, it would cost us everything that we had. Her response was, 'Go for it, and if you fail and become a beggar, I will stick by you and beg with you.' So, I put into it all our money and all the money that we could borrowed, and took over that factory. Nowadays, it produces 5 million yuan in profit every year."

Indeed, even if the vision is right, even if the numbers make sense, it still takes guts to actually pull the trigger. Looking back, he thought that the most important factor in his success was coming up with the courage to pull the trigger, buy that factory and take the risk.

Yes, entrepreneurship and investments inherently carry risks. If you invest in the stock market, the market may crash tomorrow, or next month. If you invest in real estate, the market may also crash someday, or a careless tenant may burn down the house. However, risks are everywhere. There are many car accidents every day, but people still drive. While we cannot eliminate risk, we can learn to manage, limit and minimize risk.

As people say: "Protect the downside, and the upside will take care of itself."

How to manage risk in real estate. Here is how I have tried to protect the down side in my real estate investing. Every time we bought a house as a rental property, I would estimate that after a 20% down payment, the rent and all the expenses should at least breakeven, or preferably have some positive cash-flow. If the rent income is not enough to cover the mortgage and all other expenses, then I walk away. It means that the price for that house is too high for me.

Even in recessions, people need a place to live. If some people lose their own homes, they will become renters, thus increasing the renters' pool. Therefore, there will always be demand for rental houses, even in recessions. As long as there is positive cash-flow from the rental property or at least break-even, the landlord can survive and wait out the storm to enjoy the up cycle after the recession. However, if the cash-flow is negative and the landlord has to feed money into the rental properties every month, then the rental properties could become an "alligator" that will eat the landlord alive, especially during a recession.

In addition, to protect the downside, I buy sufficient insurance to cover each rental house, plus a $3 million umbrella insurance covering all the rental houses. For the office properties, we have a liability insurance of $1 million for each occurrence and $2 million aggregate, plus $2 million umbrella insurance, for each property.

Real estate investing can be a good way to manage your risk if your job or business are in another field. Among the relatives that my wife and I have in China, there is a loving and generous couple who run a shoe manufacturing company. They have successfully operated this company for over a decade until 2-3 years ago, when the shoe manufacturing business started to decline. Too many people were doing it, and supply exceeded demand. The couple saw it coming, because they saw more and more shoe manufacturing companies being established while demand softened.

They were smart people and wanted to manage and minimize that risk. So, they made preparations in advance by pouring their profits into real estate in the form of street-front stores as rental properties. By the time the shoe manufacturing business declined significantly, they had already owned several retail properties generating a nice cash-flow.

In the summer of 2018, my wife and I visited one of their rental properties, a furniture store operated by another company that rented their space. It was a huge space on the main street, selling beautiful and luxurious furniture. My wife actually wanted to buy some of their furniture, except that it would be difficult to ship them from there to the U.S. As a result of their diversification into real estate, even if someday there might be no income from their shoe manufacturing business, they still receive more than 1 million yuan in rental income annually.

Sometimes, taking some risk is necessary in order to mitigate risk. Sometimes, bitter medicine is necessary to heal a sickness. Through the risk they took to enter into real estate investment, they have neutralized the risk from their shoe business and secured financial freedom for their family.

Make your money on Wall Street and bury it on main street. In the LK building where we own an office condo, there was another condo occupied by a company whose founder and CEO is a highly capable gentleman (I will call him Jack in this book). Jack runs a successful company, and he has used profits from his company to buy real estate to diversify. He has so far purchased a dozen commercial real estate properties within about a 30-mile radius, valued at about $3 to $12 million each.

He told me that he looked for a cap rate of at least 7-8%, put down 20-25% down payment, and the rest with loans from a local commercial bank. He said that one day every month, he has a meeting with his real estate team including an agent, an accountant, and a property manager from a management company that he has hired to manage his properties. They give him updates and reports, and he discusses with them what to do next.

His company continues to do well. However, even if in the case that some unexpected things happen that may negatively affect his company, he has mitigated his risk by burying his profits in main street, with rental properties that produce significant cash-flows.

The risks of investing vs. the risks of being an employee. This line of thinking also applies to the regular salaried worker with a full-time job. Many people think that investing is risky, while keeping a job as a full-time employee is the way to play it safe.

In reality, being an employee and avoiding the investment "risk" carries arguably more risk of its own.

Let's look at manufacturing employment in the U.S. as an example. According to the Bureau of Labor Statistics of the U.S. Department of Labor, there were two periods that saw manufacturing employment fall sharply:

From 1980 to 2000, two million manufacturing jobs were lost. From 2000 to 2017, 5.5 million manufacturing jobs were lost. (https://www.bls.gov/opub/mlr/2018/beyond-bls/the-fall-of-employment-in-the-manufacturing-sector.htm).

Indeed, the labor statistics also show that nearly 6 million American factory workers lost their jobs between year 2000 and 2010 (https://qz.com/1269172/the-epic-mistake-about-manufacturing-thats-cost-americans-millions-of-jobs/).

In addition to the decline in the manufacturing sector, you have probably seen brick-and-mortar retailers close in your area in the past several years. Across the U.S., in numerous cities and suburbs, retail stores have been having a wave of closings. According to data from Coresight Research, in 2018 alone, 5,854 stores closed their doors. In 2019, from January to mid-April, 5,994 stores had already announced their plans to close, which were more than all the store closures in the entire year of 2018 (https://www.nytimes.com/ 2019/04/12/business/retail-store-closings.html).

In particular, malls in the U.S. are being hit especially hard. According to a report from Credit Suisse, 20% to 25% of all malls in the U.S. would close in the next five years, with massive numbers of employees, including store managers, sales clerks and security guards, losing their jobs (https://www.businessinsider.com/american-retail-apocalypse-in-photos-2018-1).

How about the high-paying jobs in the financial sector? Lehman Brothers and Bear Sterns come to mind. Lehman Brothers filed for bankruptcy on September 15, 2008, and 25,000 of their employees lost their jobs. The well-known investment bank Bear Stearns imploded and was taken over by JPMorgan in March 2008.

In addition to recessions, layoffs happen in other times too. For example, Deutsche Bank announced in July 2019 (while the economy was doing well) that the bank was cutting 18,000 jobs (www.cnn.com/2019/07/08/investing/deutsche-bank-layoffs/index.html). Indeed, many people's "stable" jobs are only one company restructuring or consolidation away from being lost.

Are the highly-educated employees in the high-tech industries safer? Many employees would tell you that as they approach the ages of around 45 or 50, they fear the increased likelihood of being let go by the companies. The high-tech companies may replace them with younger and less expensive employees fresh out of universities with a new generation of high-tech knowledge and fresh cutting-edge skills.

Several years ago, not far from where I lived, a well-known tech company's branch closed its door and let go its employees, including many engineers. While the younger employees could relocate and find jobs elsewhere, many others who were 50 years of age or older found it difficult to find another job in the high-tech industry. Several years ago, another high-tech company near where we live closed a department and let go its people, my friend included. Luckily, after a few months, he was able to find another job. But that was a stressful few months for him, being the father of three kids.

Following the Great Recession of 2008-2009, from June 2009 to fall 2019 (at the writing of this book), the U.S. economy had been growing for over 125 months. This was the longest economic expansion in the U.S. history. It had surpassed the previous record of the longest expansion from

March 1991 to March 2001. Even in this record expanding economy, layoffs still happened. On October 3, 2019, for example, the Wall Street Journal reported that HP planned to cut up to 9,000 jobs in a new restructuring plan.

Besides the risks of being laid off, there is also the risk of emotional stress due to the lack of financial freedom, and the physical and emotional stress of working long hours at the job, especially when you have an unreasonable and unfriendly boss. Even if one has a high-paying job and lives a good life, without owning cash-producing assets, that good life will likely end once the paychecks stop coming.

Trading hours for dollars isn't freedom. The salary from being an employee is "active income". This is in contrast to "passive income". For example, a real estate investor can be sitting on the beach or vacationing in Europe, and the rental properties are generating cash every month. To earn active income, you have to pour in more hours of your life to get more dollars. In addition, financial ruin could be only a few missed paychecks away, whether due to layoffs or a major sickness.

It is a myth that investing is risky and being an employee is safer. The reality is quite the opposite. To reduce the risk:

(1) One can use savings from the active income (salary) to invest in assets that spit out cash every month.

(2) Then use both salary and rental property cash-flow to buy more assets that spit out cash every month.

(3) Then use salary and even more cash-flow from your rental properties to buy even more assets that spit out even more cash every month.

(4) Stay persistent and continue this virtuous cycle.

(5) Once the cash-flow from rental properties is enough for you and your family to live on, then you have minimized the risks, and have achieved freedom of money and time.

Three types of freedom. By investing in real estate and accumulate cash-producing properties, you can achieve three types of freedom.

(1) Financial freedom. There is enough money for you and your family to live on, even if you do not work. You are free from the fear of being laid off and lose your paycheck. You can choose to continue to work if you enjoy your work, or you can retire and pursue other goals in your life, such as volunteering, helping others, or touring the world.

(2) Life freedom. You do not have a boss who controls your life and orders you around. You do not have to put up with a nasty manager or supervisor. It is like what a bumper sticker says: "Retired! No boss. No hurry. No worry." You are free from the fear of your boss being unhappy with you and unsatisfied with your job performance. You are free from the bondage of unfair bosses and the fear that the company may down size and lay you off.

(3) Time freedom. I have read an interesting definition about job. What is a job? "Every morning, millions of parents are taken away from their homes and from their children, by a horrible thing called job." Time freedom means that you have plenty of time to spend with your kids, your spouse, your parents and other loved ones. In the morning, you can sleep in. And if you get up and feel like visiting a national park or a city or a museum, you just pick up your stuff and go. If you and your spouse like to take a cruise ship trip, just book some tickets and go. If you feel like learning to paint, learning to dance, or pursue other happiness in your life, you have the time freedom to do so.

"Life, Liberty and the Pursuit of Happiness" is a well-known phrase in the U.S. Declaration of Independence. The three types of freedom, described above, are fully consistent with life, liberty, and the pursuit of happiness, which you can achieve through investing in real estate.

However, as Jack Ma said to this effect: "Today, you work hard. The day after tomorrow, life will be beautiful and grand. However, tomorrow, you will go through setbacks and challenges. Many people die tomorrow and never reach the day after tomorrow." Today, you have made progress and started to acquire properties. The day after tomorrow, you will achieve the beautiful financial freedom. However, tomorrow, you may have some difficulties and setbacks, and you've got work to do. It takes courage, resilience and optimism to keep going, which will be the focus of the next chapter.

Chapter 16. Courage, Resilience, and Optimism

Do not judge me by my success, judge me by how many times I fell down and got back up again.

--Nelson Mandela

It's been eight years, and my wife and I have increased our humble net worth to $5.5 million. Our net cash-flow from rental properties reached $150,000 per year. Looking back, I feel that courage, resilience, and optimism are among the most important elements that have helped us to keep going.

The real estate investing approach described in this book is a steady, reliable, sustainable and long-term effort toward financial freedom. If you follow the preceding chapters, the methods are feasible, reproducible and not overly complicated.

However, one key factor that my experience shows to be critically important is for the investor to be courageous, resilient and optimistic. Knowing the methods is one thing; having the courage, optimism and tenacity to keep going is another.

Therefore, this book would not be complete without the current chapter. This is a long-term game. It takes persistence, patience and resilience to stay in the game. It takes courage and optimism to keep going in the face of challenges, obstacle, and at times a steep learning curve.

I have drawn strengths from the following examples; I hope that they will also inspire you and give you the tenacity and toughness to keep going in your investing journey toward financial freedom.

Courage. Sam Zell, the real estate billionaire, is nicknamed "the grave dancer". He was born in Chicago in 1941. His parents were Jewish immigrants, who made the wise decision to flee Poland just before the Nazis invaded in 1939. When Sam Zell attended the University of Michigan, he ventured into the real estate business, first as a property manager for other landlords, then as an investor himself.

After graduating from law school, Mr. Zell found a job at a blue-chip law firm in Chicago. Those who knew him well predicted that he would last for no more than three months on the job. He lasted only a week. After spending four days drafting a contract, he told his bosses that he was quitting his law job.

His bosses were of course surprised. After inquiring about the reason to quit, they were impressed by the real estate investing dream of this young confident guy. Instead of pulling his ear and showing him the door, they provided funds and became partners in his real estate investment ("Money Talks, Bullsh*t Walks", by Ben E. Johnson). Mr. Zell's courage was demonstrated in this major decision to leave the familiar and well-respected traditional path, and leave promptly, to pursue the less familiar dream in a less traveled path.

The next Monday, he bought an apartment project in Toledo, Ohio, according to https://www.bisnow.com/national/news/commercial-real-estate/behind-the-gravedancer-the-formation-story-of-real-estate-mogul-sam-zell-60865. In the crash of the 1970s, the grave dancer's audacious actions were on full display, as he made a fortune buying distressed real estate properties. He bought those nearly dead properties and resurrecting them for tens of millions in profits.

When there was blood in the streets, when others panicked, his courage enabled him to calmly analyze, discover and seize great opportunities.

According to https://knowledge.wharton.upenn.edu/article/real-estate-developer-and-grave-dancer-sam-zell-its-all-about-supply-and-demand/, following the 1973 market crash, Mr. Zell spent the next three years acquiring $3 billion in real estate assets.

He went to the banks and lenders and told them that he could buy their distressed properties where the loans had gone bad, to take the future operating losses off their books, in return for purchasing at steep discounts. He then held on to these properties long enough for the market to eventually turn into an up cycle.

He later admitted: "As it turns out, we made a fortune."

His nickname "the grave dancer" grew out of the title of an article that he wrote for the New York University Review in the 1970s. In this article, he described his courageous strategy of profiting by buying distressed real estate properties on the cheap. Zell said that the article showed how "I was dancing on the skeletons of other people's mistakes." In the doom and gloom market resembling the heavy atmosphere of a graveyard, Zell was happily dancing because he saw so many opportunities.

Just like Buffett, who, when panic was everywhere, was "tap dancing to work" to buy stocks at a substantial discount. When panic descends and "the sky is falling", courageous investors focus on the cold hard numbers and seize the rare opportunities.

Resilience. My daughter was seriously ill and hospitalized for 21 days in 2010; thank God she later fully recovered. I found it inspiring to read about the experience of Charlie Munger, Warren Buffett's billionaire partner. As recorded in "The Snowball" (Alice Schroeder, page 199), in 1953, Mr. Munger's marriage was not working, and they were divorcing due to incompatibility, fighting and misery. Mr. Munger moved out of the house. A year later, they eight-year-old son was diagnosed with leukemia. The disease was incurable, and it was deeply painful to watch the child suffer and deteriorate day by day. Mr. Munger often held his son in his arms and walked the streets, weeping. The combination of the failed marriage, having moved out and living alone, and his son's terminal illness was as heavy as a mountain on his heart.

This was when Mr. Munger's resilience showed. In this misery and heart-broken situation, he was determined to pursue new goals, instead of dwelling in the negative thoughts. He said: "You should never, when facing some unbelievable tragedy, let one tragedy increase into two or three through your failure of will."

While caring for his dying son, he decided to get married again. He married his current wife in 1956, and in the subsequent years, they increased the family size with a daughter and three sons. Munger would later meet and befriend Buffett, and become the Vice President of Berkshire Hathaway. In the process, he became a well-known billionaire and a well-respected philanthropist.

Buffett himself is also a resilient fellow. For example, in 2000, during a physical checkup, a colonoscopy revealed an issue. Alice Schroeder described this in "Snowball" (page 581) with such good humor that it's worth quoting here: "A sizeable benign polyp was nesting in his gut. The polyp had taken over so much real estate that removing it would require demolishing a good chunk of the surrounding neighborhood. It had a few small friends nearby as well." The doctors spent several hours to perform the surgery. They removed fifteen inches of his intestine and left him with a seven-inch scar. This was nothing to sneeze at. However, during the subsequent week recovering in bed at home, Buffett was already cracking jokes on the phone with friends:

"I'm not tired at all, I'm perfectly fine. Did I tell you that the anesthesiologist used to be my caddy at the country club? I told him before he put me under that I sure hope I tipped him well." "By the way, did I tell you that I went into the hospital with a colon, but I came out with a semicolon?"

After the surgery, while others may be worried about the health, the healing and recovery process, and the possibility of infection, Buffett showed his tough resilience. He was consumed with an optimistic mood and good sense or humor. He was filled with positive thinking and beamed with buoyant cheerfulness. Such a resilience in a setback would be a highly beneficial character to help the investor persist, sustain, and succeed.

When you start your real estate investing journey, there will be setbacks in life as well as in investments. There will be times when you have self-doubts and feel like quitting. I hope that you, too, can draw strengths from the experience of Munger and Buffett. Instead of dwelling in negative thoughts, set new goals and continue your real estate journey, and be resilient and persistent long enough to be rewarded with your financial freedom.

Optimism. In 1974, the U.S. economy was in deep trouble and the inflation was at 11%. The prices of the famous nifty-fifty stocks dropped by 80%. From 1968 to 1974, the general stock market had gone down by 70%. The prolonged bear market was in its sixth year by the time 1974 arrived.

People were scared and worn out, and had stopped buying stocks. Stock market experts were advising people to postponing the purchase of stocks, "until there is more certainty." ("Buffett", by Roger Lowenstein, page 161.)

This was when Buffett's optimism shone. In October 1974, he had an interview with *Forbes*. Against the backdrop of "The sky is falling", Buffett declared: "This is the time to start investing", this is the time to load up your truck. His confidence and optimism enabled him to publicly declare to *Forbes* in the doom and gloom of 1974: "Now is the time to invest and get rich!"

More recently, during the financial tsunami of 2008, Fannie Mae and Freddie Mac failed and were taken over by the government. AIG nearly went under and had to be bailed out by the U.S. government. Lehman Brothers went into bankruptcy. With his typical optimism when optimism was in short supply, Buffett went on TV to stress the need for confidence. He published an editorial in New York Times that entitled, "Buy America: I Am."

During the crisis, his optimistic and calm words spread worldwide like a cool stream of water in the scorching desert. And here are some of his bold actions in the market crash and its subsequent years: He poured $5 billion into Goldman Sachs, and $5 into Bank of America. He spent $34 billion to buy Burlington Northern Santa Fe Railway in 2009. Buffett's optimism, confidence and courage have made him one of the richest people in the world and one of the best investors of all time.

I like to read the biographies of successful people. Many successful people appear to share one important character: They have a strongly optimistic attitude, they think positively, and they express uplifting messages.

While contemplating on this interesting phenomenon, I realized that, the future is never clear, and no one can predict with certainty what will happen tomorrow, let alone next month or next year. There may be a war. There may be a terrorist attack. There may be an earthquake, a hurricane, a fire, or a plaque.

Therefore, it takes a strong optimism to invest into the future. This is especially true in a crisis, when your friends, colleagues and family members are scared to invest. However, that is when assets are on sale and buying opportunities are abundant.

In such dire, dark and desperate moments, a pessimist would be too worried about the future to invest, thereby missing the opportunities.

No wonder many successful people are usually optimistic, resilient, confident, and passionate. While highly analytical and independent, they also have a good sense of humor. In contrast, a pessimist tends to see the worst aspect of things or believe that the worst will happen.

The reality is, a pessimist tends to not dare to pour money into investments, because tomorrow is not certain, the future is never clear, and investments carry risks. The market may crash in the near future, the rental property may go up in flames, and there may be natural disasters that destroy the rental properties. So, a pessimist would wait, worry, and hesitate, while missing the previous window of opportunity.

People would agree that if you burn 100 of your $100 bills into ashes, you have lost $10k. But many do not realize that the missed opportunities could mean losing a lot more than $10k.

People say "cash is king." I have put together the following which I think is more accurate, and I call it CCCK:

Cash + Crisis + Courage = King.

I have also put together the following to show the point:

Optimism + Careful Analysis + Courage = Wealth.

Pessimism = Lost Opportunities = Burning Cash.

In addition, as a compounding factor, optimism also helps you to build a productive team and establish a fruitful network. Buffett described Charlie Munger as someone who would roll on the floor laughing at his own jokes; the two became partners because "That's my kind of guy."

Being optimistic attracts people. People like to be around an optimistic person. Just ask yourself: Do you prefer your boss, partner or friend to be gloomy and pessimistic? Or do you prefer them to be optimistic and uplifting, and have a good sense of humor?

Optimism has enabled Buffett to pierce through the gloomy dark fog and see the bright future. Optimism has given him the courage to pour his money into the market when others were scared. Optimism has enabled him to load up his truck when others were dumping in panic. Optimism also has contributed to Munger's becoming Buffett's friend and partner, and to his success and growth into a billionaire.

I hope that this chapter will inspire you to strive to be an optimistic, courageous, resilient, and successful investor. And then, the next chapter will balance courage with caution; courage and caution are the two wings that allow you, the investor eagle, to soar high and fly well.

Chapter 17. Tell Me Where I'm Going to Die So I'll Never Go There

You have to stick within what I call your circle of competence. You have to know what you understand and what you don't understand. It's not terribly important how big the circle is. But it is terribly important that you know where the perimeter is.

-- Charlie Munger

Courage and optimism are not blind. A successful investor needs to be not only courageous and optimistic, but also cautious, careful, and good at common sense analysis to possess a competitive edge. The combination of the current chapter with the preceding chapter provides the needed balance and makes the picture complete.

Paying too much. One of the ways an investor can make a major mistake is paying too much for an investment. If you fall in love with a real estate property, and in the heat and emotion of a bidding war, it is easy to pay too much in order to grab that property. However, as they say: "You make your money when you buy, not when you sell." It is critically important to buy only when the price is right.

I remember two townhouses several years ago that I walked away from, and I am glad I did. The first was a well-decorated townhouse with a deck and a detached two-car garage, that we kind of fell in love with. And the sellers were a very nice couple. We offered $295k and our offer was accepted. After cooling off for a day, I realized that I offered too much. I could buy a similar townhouse with $15k to $20k less. However, I felt embarrassing to tell my agent to withdraw our offer, and I felt bad because the sellers were friendly people. Eventually, I reminded myself that price was a key factor and I needed to be disciplined. We walked away and later bought another townhouse at a much better price.

In the second case, we were looking at an end-unit townhouse that was previously a model home of the builder. It was painted and decorated beautifully and drew a lot of attention. Several potential buyers were looking at this house, including a lady investor whom we knew and were kind of in competition with. The self-pride told me to grab this house and show them that I was the winner. I offered $290k and my offer was accepted.

Again, later, my sense and discipline came back. I knew in my gut that I was over-paying in order to prove myself and impress the others, and that I could find a similar townhouse to buy and save $20k, without the beautiful wall painting, but with a similar rental income nonetheless. I was able to walk away quickly and correct my mistake. I hope that these experiences will also help you and remind you to avoid paying too much.

Paying too much will hurt the profit; as a result, there may be little or no cash-flow, or even negative cash-flow. These factors, month after month, will hurt your appetite to invest and quench your enthusiasm to buy more properties. Therefore, keep your sharp focus on the numbers, and when the numbers do not meet your criteria, walk away and keep looking. Avoid paying too much for something you want.

Over-leverage. I know a local well-known real estate broker who had a large team of agents, numerous customers, and substantial commission income. He used the commission income to buy large and relatively luxurious single houses as rental properties. During the peak of his career, he owned quite a few single houses in various parts of the state, and several beautiful beach houses. His cash-flow was negative because the rent was not enough to cover the mortgages and other expenses for these luxurious single houses. However, that was fine with him because he had substantial commission income to feed into these negative cash-flow properties.

Then, the housing market cooled and his commission income declined. His real estate brokerage company got into some internal fights and legal troubles. His income diminished and he was unable to feed the negative cash-flow properties any more. Eventually, he defaulted on the mortgages, lost the houses, and declared bankruptcy. I do not wish this on anyone. I hope that he has learned the lesson and I wish him well. I hope that this example will help you to avoid over-leveraging, avoid the negative cash-flow "alligators", and remember "Tell me where I going to die so that I'll never go there".

As you can see, if his properties had positive cash-flow, or at least were breaking even (meaning that rental income was enough to cover mortgages and all other expenses), he would not have had to default on the mortgages and losing the houses to the lenders. He could have held on to these properties, waited out the storm and waited for the next up cycle of the market.

Therefore, to be on the safe side, my wife and I have insisted on a significant positive cash-flow for our rental properties.

Another note here: In my area, if you buy large and relatively luxurious single houses as rental properties, with 20% down payment, it is difficult to break even, let alone achieving positive cash-flow.

For example, based on the past several years in my area, a $300k townhouse can command a $2,000/month rent. However, a $600k detached single house can command only $3,000/month rent, and a $900k big single house can only command about $4,000/month rent.

In comparison, if you buy three townhouses at $300k each (costing $900k), your rent income would be $6,000/month, much higher than $4,000/month in the case of the big single house. In addition, the smaller $300k townhouses will have less vacancy than the $900k big house, because the vast majority of renters cannot afford, or do not want, to pay the $4,000/month rent. They would rather rent a townhouse and pay $2,000/month.

The following are the reasons that I have focused on buying townhouses as rental properties than big detached single family homes or luxurious houses: (1) greater cash-flow; (2) better rate of return on the invested capital; (3) easier to find tenants with less vacancy.

Conclusions here: (1) Do not over-leverage; (2) have positive cash-flow or at least break even; (3) buy relatively small houses as rental properties and avoid large and luxurious houses.

Entering into unfamiliar territory. Warren Buffett says that he stays inside his "Circle of Competence". He would draw a circle around himself and stay inside it where he is the known top expert and has a competitive edge.

I draw a tiny humble circle of competence for myself, and I stay within this circle. This circle includes the townhouses within a couple of miles of radius from where I live, and the nearby office market (thanks to my mentor LK).

I know someone who is a homeowner and has a couple of rental houses. She bought a parcel of land with $250,000 cash, and planned to develop that land and build some houses to make a profit. After she bought the land, she brought an architect and a civil engineer to look at the land to get things started. Unfortunately, after some research, they told her that this land has soil problems and ground issues. It cannot be developed and won't receive permits from the government. The last time I spoke with her, she had held that land for a decade, unable to develop it and unable to sell it.

Meanwhile, if she had had used that $250,000 cash as down payment to buy three townhouses with leverage as rental properties, that $250,000 would have more than tripled. Even if she had simply put that money into an S&P 500 index fund, it would have more than doubled in the past decade.

The fact is, she is one of the smartest persons that I know of. She has a PhD degree and is highly intelligent. She is well-respected within her circle of expertise. She has been a homeowner and rental house landlord. So, she knows houses well. Yet, land development was outside her circle of competence.

My mentor LK knows someone who bought several connected parcels of land near a street with the plan of building a dozen townhouses. After he bought these connected parcels, he started the development. Unfortunately, he found out that he had missed something. There was quite a distance to connect the sewage lines, gas lines and pipes to the main street. These additional works would cost him almost a million dollars extra. However, he did not have that extra money. And this extra cost would have rendered this deal unprofitable anyway, because this surprising cost was not included in his expenses estimate. He had used the land as collateral to get a loan from the bank to buy this land; he needed to build and sell the townhouses to pay back the loan. Not only did he not have the money to complete the needed underground work for this land, but also that this unexpected extra work would substantially delay the process of building the townhouses. This meant that he had to carry the loan and pay the monthly mortgages much longer, with no end in sight due to the lack of funds to get the job started. Eventually, he had to declare bankruptcy.

Whatever you invest in, be it land development, apartment buildings, or shopping centers, there are a hundred details that are important, that require expertise, and that can go wrong. It pays to avoid entering into investments that are outside of your circle of competence.

If the investment opportunity is outside your circle of competence, no matter how exciting or promising it is, no matter how beautiful the advertisement is, promptly walk away. It is a like a competition; if you are not the expert, then you do not have a competitive edge, and the other guy is going to win. It will save you a lot of money and headache to stay inside your circle of competence.

Putting everything into one big building. If you invest in commercial properties such as office buildings and apartment buildings, it is important to avoid putting all your money into one big building. Imagine if you have all, or the majority of, your funds in one big office building, and then the economy happens to get hit by a recession and some tenant companies close their doors, and your mortgage comes due. For example, if the loan has a 6-year maturity with 25-year amortization, then the loan needs to be reviewed and approved for renewal by the lender every six years. If your building has lost some or many tenants, during a recession, lenders often refuse to renew the loan. Then you will need to pay off the outstanding debt, which is likely several million dollars for your building. In such cases, investors often are either forced to sell the building on the cheap, or default and lose the building to the lender.

In contrast, imagine that you have your funds invested in several smaller buildings (for example, instead of owning a single $15 million building, you own five buildings worth $3 million for each building). Three factors will be in your favor.

(1) Since you buy these five buildings gradually over the years, your five loans will mature in different years; they will not mature all at the same time. Therefore, only one loan will mature during a recession, which is a much smaller loan amount than that in the case of one big $15 million building.

(2) Statistically, perhaps only one of your five buildings (20% of the properties) will turn negative cash-flow in a

recession, while the other four buildings will still have positive cash-flow due to rent increases and paying down your mortgages in the past years. In a recession, depending on the severity and location, usually only 5% to 20% of commercial properties will get into trouble. If you have one big building and you happen to be among those 5% to 20%, it will sink your ship. However, if you have diversified into, say, five buildings, then the statistics will be in your favor, and you will still have the other four positive cash-flow buildings to bail out the one negative cash-flow building.

(3) If you have diversified into five buildings, when each loan becomes mature, each lender will be more likely to agree to renew your loan, because each loan is a smaller loan, and the lender will see that you have a number of other properties (with a number of years still remaining before maturity) producing positive cash-flow.

Therefore, a general guideline is that you should have no more than 10-20% of your wealth invested in one single building.

Old properties and old neighborhoods. The U.S. infrastructure is getting old with some underground gas lines that are 60-80 years old. If you watch the news and search the internet, you will find cases of gas leaks causing explosions, demolishing houses and buildings, and injuring or even killing people. For a pension fund or a major insurance company that owns, for example, 100 apartment buildings all over the country, they can survive an old gas line leak causing an explosion that demolishing one apartment building. They have billions of dollars and the other 99 apartment buildings still spitting out major cash for them.

However, for a small investor like me, such an explosion can sink us. Even if there is good liability insurance and umbrella insurances in place, families of the injured and the killed tenants will sue the owners and the lawsuits will drag on for a long time, while the demolished apartments will not be spitting out cash.

Another factor is that buildings that are a hundred years old may have hidden structural issues that may be difficult to find. Unless you are an expert on analyzing century-old buildings and this is within your circle of competence, it is better to stay away. I have looked at several properties that are around a century old with very good cap rates, and it was tempting. I talked to my insurance agent who takes care of all my properties. She advised against purchasing such old buildings, as she has seen very old structures that can have catastrophic problems, which can sink the small investor.

Granted, if you have the required expertise and you are familiar with and confident in investing in old buildings and old neighborhoods, you can do well. But old buildings and old neighborhoods are an extra complication, and a small new investor needs to respect that complication. For me, there are plenty of newer real estate properties in newer neighborhood to invest in. If you are a small investor, and especially if you are a beginner, it would be beneficial to stick with newer and simpler properties.

Albert Einstein was quoted to have ranked the level of intelligence this way:

1. Smart;
2. Intelligent;
3. Genius;
4. Simple.

In this ranking, "Simple" is the highest level of intelligence. Perhaps Einstein was thinking about his famous simple formula: $E = mc^2$, when he put together this intelligence ranking with "Simple" at the highest intelligence level.

Therefore, in your investing, keep it simple. If the soundness of the ageing structure of the building is in doubt, or if the safety of the old gas lines underground is a concern, just walk away. If it's one big attractive building but you feel that it would be too complicated to figure a way out in case of a recession, or if it is a beautiful parcel of bare land but you don't know much about developing a piece of land, walk away.

There are always more opportunities than your money. It's prudent to let go some risky opportunities. If your expertise is simply townhouses and small single houses, you can still do very well in real estate investing.

Stay in your circle of competence, avoid the overly complicated, and keep it simple. This way, you are practicing "Tell me where I'm going to die so I'll never go there."

Besides the pitfalls described in this chapter, another reason that may stop you from pursuing your financial freedom is that: "I am forty years old. I am fifty years old. It's too late to start investing in real estate." This issue will be addressed in the next chapter.

Chapter 18. Better Late Than Never

Today is your youngest day in the rest of your life.

-- Unknown

If you are reading this book in your twenties or thirties, congratulations! You are getting a head start in the right direction. However, don't worry if you are older. As a scientist buried in research for decades, I myself started late investing in real estate, when I was 47. I hope that the following examples will give you courage and inspiration.

Buffett made 99.6% of his money after the age of 52. I read the biographies "Buffett: The Making of an American Capitalist" (by Roger Lowenstein) and "The Snowball – Warren Buffett and the Business of Life" (by Alice Schroeder). I also searched sources www.marketwatch.com/story/from-6000-to-67-billion-warren-buffetts-wealth-through-the-ages-2015-08-17, and https://medium.com/the-10x-entrepreneur/warren-buffett-has-made-99-7-of-his-money-after-the-age-of-52-71e2ce04c347. I went through the Berkshire Hathaway Annual Reports for the past decades.

Indeed, Mr. Warren Buffett made 99.6% of his wealth after his 52nd birthday (see figure below).

How is this possible? Don't people think that 52 is kind of late, and that you should have made the bulk of your wealth by then already? How did he make the bulk (99.6%) of his wealth after 52? Does this mean that, if we are already 40 or 50, that it is not too late for us to start investing?

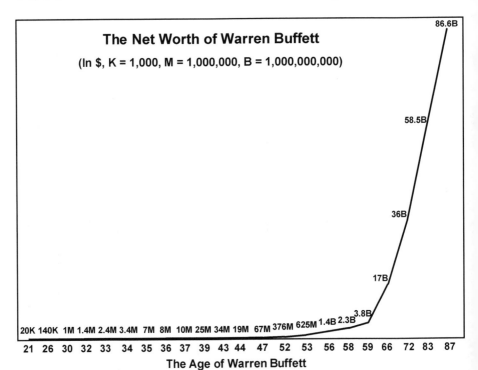

The Net Worth of Warren Buffett

(In \$, K = 1,000, M = 1,000,000, B = 1,000,000,000)

The Age of Warren Buffett

At the age of 52, Buffett's wealth was \$376 million (= \$0.376 billion). At 87, his wealth was \$86.6 billion. There are 35 years from 52 to 87. \$86.6 billion / \$0.376 billion = 1.1683^{35}.

126

Therefore, by growing at an average compound rate of 16.83% annually in the past 35 years, his wealth went from $0.376 billion to $86.6 billion.

You may have noticed that different rates of return have been quoted for Buffett. This is because the time range is different in the different examples. This example used a time range of 35 years from his age of 52 to 87. Another example used a time range of 1965-2018. Another example used a time range of 2011-2019, and so on.

With an increase from $0.376 billion to $86.6 billion (as of 2018), (86.6 − 0.376)/86.6 = 99.6%. Therefore, by compounding at a rate of 16.83% annually, Buffett made 99.6% of his money after the age of 52.

My wife and I made 85% of our wealth in the last 8 years after I was 47. In our humble example of increasing our wealth from $0.8 million to $5.5 million in 8 years: (5.5-0.8)/5.5 = 85%. Hence, in our case:

(1) We made 15% of our wealth in two decades of working hard at our jobs from our late twenties to age 47;

(2) We made 85% of our wealth from age of 47 to 55 through real estate investing.

Therefore, you can still make the bulk of your wealth in investing even if you start late.

Here are other factors that may help erase your concerns and increase your confidence. (1) I am not handy and not physically strong; (2) I spend 50+ hours per week on a busy job; (3) I live in a relatively slow or normal housing price appreciation market; (4) My wife and I have raised three kids and paid for their college tuitions with 0 student loans; (5) We sent money to help parents and relatives.

Therefore, I truly believe that if we can do it, you can too.

The real estate investing returns that my wife and I achieved, which are based on annual housing price appreciations of 3-5% as shown in previous chapters, can be reasonably achieved and duplicated by others. Furthermore, very importantly, these real estate investing returns are sustainable in the long-term, because they were achieved in a normal market with appreciation rates similar to the historic long-term average. They were not achieved in a booming housing market that may last for only a few years and cannot be sustained in the long-term.

Therefore, I would like to emphasize the following main points here. If you study this book and other related books, and practice the methods and approaches described in this book:

(1) You should be able to achieve an annual rate of return of 15% to 20%.

(2) You can build substantial cash-flow every month and achieve financial freedom, even if you are already in your 40s and 50s.

(3) The younger you are when you start, the better. Remember the 8th wonder of the world. Pull the trigger, get started, and do not wait.

(4) The age of 50 is not the end. It is not even the beginning of the end. It is only the end of the beginning.

Emphasis: Our returns were not achieved in a hot housing market during the boom years. A housing price appreciation of 3-5% annually, which my rental properties experienced, does not deviate from the long-term historic average in my area. Our rate of return was not achieved by someone who lived in a fast-growing market with rapid housing price appreciations like 8% or 12% annually, such as Seattle, San Francisco, Denver, and Houston in the past several years.

For example, according to www.propertyradar.com/blog/its-not-a-housing-bubble-san-francisco-bay-area-housing-market, from February 2016 to February 2017, the San Francisco Bay Area Median Price for single family residence increased by 12.8% in a year.

In Seattle, according to Case Shiller home price index, single-family-home prices for the Seattle metro area increased by 12.7% in a year, from December 2016 to December 2017 (https://www.seattletimes.com/business/real-estate/seattle-area-home-market-was-nations-hottest-for-2017/).

These high rates of housing price appreciation likely cannot be sustained in the long-term, and cannot be reproduced in most parts of the country, where the housing price appreciation is closer to the U.S. national average.

National average housing price appreciation in the past 44 years. According to the "Economic Research" published by the Federal Reserve Bank of St. Lois (https://fred.stlouisfed.org/series/USSTHPI), the "All-Transactions House Price Index for the United States" shows a housing price index of 61 for 1975, and 444 for 2019. There are 44 years from 1975 to 2019. $444/61 = 1.046^{44}$, or 4.6% annually in average.

There have been ups and downs and stagnant years. But in the long-term, the housing price appreciation rate has averaged approximately 4.6% annually in the U.S. from 1975 to 2019.

Case Shiller national average housing price appreciation in the past 31 years. Case Shiller's housing price index for the national average indicates an index of approximately 65 in 1987, and 200 for 2018. There are 31 years. $200/65 = 1.037^{31}$. Therefore, the Case Shiller national average housing price increase is 3.7% per year in the period 1987-2018.

My neighborhood's average housing price appreciation in the past 20 years. In my neighborhood, the builders started to build the townhouses in 1999. The sale price then was around $200k for a typical townhouse. At the writing of this book in 2019, typical townhouses are selling for about $340k to $400k, with an average of around $370k. It has been 20 years. $370,000/200,000 = 1.032^{20}$.

Therefore, the average housing price appreciation in my neighborhood has been approximately 3.2% per year in the past two decades.

Below are the housing price appreciations per year of some of my townhouses:

Townhouse PH: See Chapter 2; the average housing price appreciation was 4.6% (It was a short sale and we purchased it at below the market price; that's why its appreciation is above the neighborhood average.)

Annual Real Estate Price Appreciation

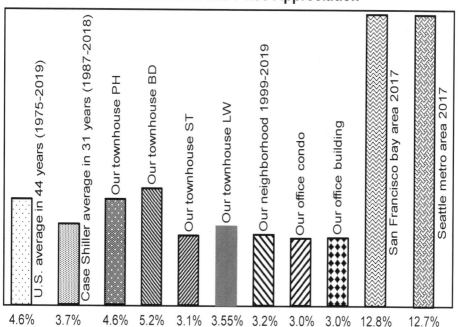

U.S. average in 44 years (1975-2019)	Case Shiller average in 31 years (1987-2018)	Our townhouse PH	Our townhouse BD	Our townhouse ST	Our townhouse LW	Our neighborhood 1999-2019	Our office condo	Our office building	San Francisco bay area 2017	Seattle metro area 2017
4.6%	3.7%	4.6%	5.2%	3.1%	3.55%	3.2%	3.0%	3.0%	12.8%	12.7%

Townhouse BD: See Chapter 3; the average housing price appreciation was 5.2% (It had extensive basement damage and we got a good deal at about $20k below the market; that's why its appreciation is above the neighborhood average.)

Townhouse ST: It is an end unit backing to a strip of forest. We purchased it for $300,000 and settled on June 5, 2014. Its basement was unfinished; after the settlement, we put in about $7000 to finish the basement. Therefore, the effective purchase price was $307,000. It has been 5 years. Its current market price is about $355,000. $355,000/307,000 = 1.031^5$. This represents an average housing price appreciation of 3.1%.

Townhouse LW: It's a townhouse with a 2-car garage. We purchased it for $320,000 and settled on May 10, 2016. We put in about $5000 to change the HVAC system, so the effective price was $325,000. It's been three years. The current price is about $360,000. $360,000/325,000 = 1.0355^3$. This indicates an average housing price appreciation of 3.55% per year in the past three years.

The main points here are:

(1) I am not one of those "gurus" who happens to be investing in a hot housing market during several boom years and then writes a book about the exciting returns. You read those books and are very impressed with the amazing results, only to find out that they cannot be reproduced in your area during your timeframe.

(2) My neighborhood actually lagged slightly behind the U. S. national average in housing price appreciation in the past 8 years. However, our results were still very good after using proper leverage and negotiation methods, as described in this book. Therefore, you can still do well following my methods, even if you do not live in a booming local market.

(3) The real estate investing and cash-flow results, described in this book, are sustainable in the long-term. This is because these results were not achieved in a short-lived booming period that will likely be followed with a down-trend or a stagnant period. Instead, our wealth accumulation and cash-flow were achieved in a normal neighborhood housing price appreciation similar to the long-term U. S. national average.

(4) Therefore, the real estate investing and cash-flow results, described in this book, are expected to be reproducible by other people.

(5) By using the acquisition and negotiation methods described in previous chapters, you can obtain a purchase price below the market, thus yielding an appreciation rate for your rental houses that is above your neighborhood average.

Emphasis: What we have achieved, you can too. I started investing in real estate on the side when I was 47 years old. My wife and I have been raising three kids and sending them to college. We have no inheritance and we have financial responsibilities like others; form example, we have been donating to church and helping relatives in need. Eight years later, the net positive cash-flow from our rentals reached $150,000 per year. We have achieved financial freedom. If we can do it, you can too. If you are currently aged around 40 or 50, it is not too late at all to get started.

Even if you start late, better late than never. If you study this book, learn from other investors, and persistently invest in real estate for 10 years, you will be pleasantly surprised and become secure financially.

If you start relatively young and persist in real estate investing for 20 years, you should be able to achieve excellent results and wonderful financial freedom for yourself and for your loved ones, as will be illustrated in the next chapter.

Chapter 19. Pursuing the Right Direction Is More Important Than Running Fast

Charlie and I have not learned how to solve difficult business problems. What we have learned to do is to avoid them. To the extent that we have been successful, it is because we concentrate on identifying one-foot hurdles that we can step over rather than because we have acquired any ability to clear seven-footers. ... It's just not necessary to do extraordinary things to get extraordinary results.

-- Warren Buffett

I have many friends, and know many others, who work really hard. Some of them spend hours commuting to work. Many of them spend long hours at the job, even working in the evenings and on the weekends. Many juggle busy jobs, family duties, kids' activities, or caring for a sick relative. The hours that they spend at work are long and stressful, and they are intelligent and productive employees. Yet many live paycheck to paycheck, many feel the financial anxiety, and many are only a company restructuring and downsizing away from financial ruin.

Buying 26 rental properties in 20 years? I once read an article about a schoolteacher who bought 26 rental properties in 20 years. The cash flow made her financially free. She retired in her early 40s to travel the world. Based on our own experience of accumulating 14 rental properties in 8 years with $150,000 cash-flow annually, it is certainly possible to accumulate 26 rental properties in 20 years and then retire.

A powerful virtuous cycle. Most people think that it is impossible to save enough income from your salary to buy 26 rental properties in 20 years. They are right.

What they fail to realize, however, is that you do not rely on your salary alone; a large portion comes from cash-flow from the rental properties. And this portion becomes larger and larger when you accumulate more and more rental properties.

Savings from salaries enable you to buy the first few rental properties. Later on, cash-flow from rental properties plays an increasingly bigger role when you save for a down payment to buy the next property.

The key here is that rental properties produce cash-flow, and cash-flow increases over the years due to rent increases. The cash-flow enables you to buy more rental properties, which in turn generate more cash, which in turn enables you to buy more cash-producing properties. Therefore, they feed on each other and turn into a powerful virtuous cycle.

In addition, the important point here is not the exact number of rental properties. Even if the teacher in the story had accumulated only 20 or 16 rental properties, they would still have allowed her to achieve financial freedom and retire early. The important point here is to persist and not give up, and to continue for many years. This is not a get-rich-quick strategy. This is a steady, reliable, sustainable and reproducible strategy to achieve financial freedom.

Start now to pursue your financial freedom. My wife and I started our real estate investing journey late, after our daughter's sickness gave us a wakeup call. We wished that we had had a chance to read a book such as this one in our 20s or 30s and started this real estate investing journey earlier.

Starting earlier would mean earlier financial freedom, earlier release from stress and anxiety, earlier enhancement of quality of life, earlier retirement, and more wealth due to more years of compounding which can make a big difference.

We have many friends who work long hours at their companies, and who spend 2-3 hours commuting daily on busy roads fighting traffic jams. We have friends who are not happy with their jobs, who have to endure high stress levels and put up with unpleasant bosses and unfair treatments. We have had quite a few friends in the past years who lost their jobs and had to search for months or even years to find another job. If they can start as early as possible, invest in real estate persistently for ten years, they can achieve financial freedom.

I wish that I has read a book like this one and started investing in real estate much earlier. If ten years ago, my friends had read a book like this one and invested in real estate, they would be in much better financial shape, and they would have reach their financial freedom.

I hope that this book will help those who are searching for a better life to start now:

(1) To see the real estate investing direction described in this book,

(2) To be motivated and encouraged by our humble real-life examples,

(3) To know how to pursue this direction, pull the trigger and get started,

(4) To achieve financial freedom and time freedom,

(5) To be freed from the stress of a busy job, and

(6) To be freed from the risk of losing a job and the financial damage to the family.

Starting early is advantageous because you could have more years for compounding to work. However, it's never too late to get started. Some people wait for 5 years and then wonder: "Why did I not start 5 years ago? I wish I had started earlier." So, the key is to start now. Now is the right time.

A possible timeline for you to accumulate rental properties. The following is a hypothetical but certainly feasible scenario and timeline that you can potentially mimic, by putting yourself into the shoes of that courageous and persistent schoolteacher who accumulated 26 rental properties in 20 years.

To buy her first property, it probably takes her, say, three years to accumulate the down payment, and maybe to buy a small 2-bedroom condo. It may take her another three years to accumulate the down payment to buy her second property, and then another three years to buy her third property.

With initially small, but gradually growing, cash-flow from the rental income, in addition to her salary, she is then able to accumulate cash faster, and to buy a rental property every two years. She may shift to small townhouses instead of condos. After a few more years, with greater cash-flow due to rent increases and acquiring more properties that spit out more cash every month, she is then able to buy a property every 1.5 years.

This puts her into a powerful virtuous cycle, in which more rent income enables her to buy more properties, and more properties spit out more cash to enable her to buy even more properties, and so on. After several more years, she can buy one property every year.

Those properties that she bought ten years ago still have similar monthly mortgage payments, but the rents have increased significantly in ten years. With further rent increases and a larger number of properties producing cash, she is able to buy two properties every year. After, say, 15 years, rents have increased substantially, especially for her earlier properties, while her mortgage payments remain nearly the same. This further increases her cash-flow. Furthermore, she has substantial equity in her early properties that she can do cash-out refinances. Therefore, she is able to buy three properties every year.

Eventually, after 20 years of persistence and focusing on her goal, she has accumulated 26 rental properties, and her cash-flow has far exceeded her salary, allowing her to retire and pursue her dream of touring the world. Over time, her cash-flow will further increase, due to gradual rent increases, and paying off the mortgages. In addition, the values of her 26 properties will increase due to appreciation.

Various ways to make money and support one's family. There are different ways to make a living. People make money via:

1. Physical labor (such as construction workers and farm laborers);

2. Technical skills (for example, plumbers and car mechanics);

3. Brain labor (including computer experts, engineers and scientists);

4. Using your money to breed more money (investors);

5. Using other people's money to breed more money (using leverage).

(Not looking down on anyone, as my father was a physical laborer, and I'm a brain laborer.)

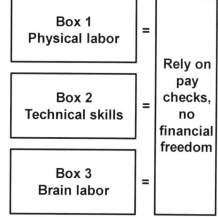

Most people belong to boxes 1-3, either without 4 or 5, or with insignificant amounts of 4 or 5 that do not allow them to be financially free. They rely on paychecks, and they will get into financial trouble if the paychecks stop, whether due to company downsizing, economic recession, or a major sickness.

The gentleman who fixed my windows (JC) told me that he had a friend who worked as a laborer to repair houses. He spent years and saved enough money (about $150k), then he used this cash to buy a small old run-down house. He spent a couple of months to put in his sweat equity, and fixed and renovated the house. Then he sold it for a nice profit, increasing his initial $150k to almost $180k. The he looked for another house to renovate and sell for a profit. After repeating this several times, with his money growing, he later did two houses simultaneously, hiring someone to do some of the work. Eventually he became the manager and mostly had others doing the renovation details for him. With his money further growing, he started to keep some of these renovated houses as rental properties. Gradually, he built a steady stream of cash-flow. He has gone from box 1 to box 4. While I did not ask JC about whether his friend used leverage, he has the option to use his houses as collateral with lenders to pull money out of these houses to buy more properties (which means going from box 1 to 5).

I have a neighbor MK who quit his accounting job years ago, and now owns twenty rental properties. I meet him often when I take a walk in the neighborhood. He would be holding a cup of coffee and walking a huge black dog. MK told me that when he had accumulated enough properties with cash-flow exceeding his accountant salary, he quit his job. He found out that I was doing real estate investing when he saw that the LK office condo was sold, and he searched the public record and found out that his neighbor, me, bought that property. He told

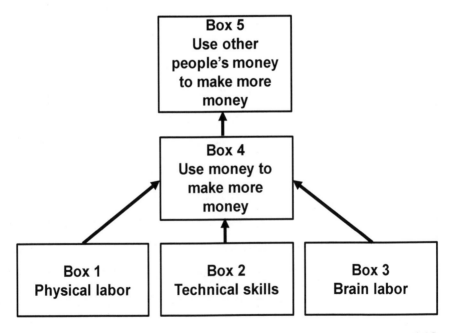

me that he has loans in many of his twenty rental properties, but they cash-flow really well. He enjoys a semi-retired life, spending a few hours a week on his "real estate empire". He is a good example of someone who has gone from box 3 to boxes 4 and 5.

I have a friend whose husband is a medical doctor. They have two lovely kids. She quit her computer job a decade ago to partly take care of the kids and partly invest in real estate. They live in a university town and her properties are mostly rented to students. He made the salary and she used the savings from the salary to pour into real estate. Then she combined salary savings with the cash-flow from the rental properties to buy more properties. This yielded even more cash-flow, which enabled her to buy even more properties.

Over the years she has accumulated dozens of rental houses near the campus, and at this writing, she has more than 100 active leases. She said that summer is busy for her because students come and go in the summer. But during the rest of the year, she is semi-retired and has a lot of time for herself and her family. She is the one who told me to use HELOC cash to buy houses in the winter, then use cash-flow to pay back the HELOC until the next winter comes.

Last time, I joked with her: "You are likely making a lot more money than your husband's salary, because salaries increase by perhaps only 3% to 5% per year, while your investment is probably compounding at 20% per year." She happily agreed.

Of course, her husband's salary was the seed money, without which she wouldn't have done so well. This is a good example of a husband-wife synergistic team, going together from box 3 to boxes 4 and 5.

Most people are not born into a level where "Rich people do not work for money. Money works for them." However, with the investment strategies and real-life methods described in this book, a small potato like me (and many others, including you) can gradually move to boxes 4 and 5. Then even we can say:

"I do not need to work for money anymore, because money works for me."

Planting your "money trees". People say: "Money doesn't grow on trees." Well, if you plant "money trees", then money does grow on "trees". Rental properties that produce cash-flows are "money trees". Even if initially your rental house only breaks even and does not yield a cash-flow, continue to nurture this tree. After some time, rents will increase and your loan amount will decrease, turning it into a cash-producing money tree. Alternatively, once you have accumulated significant equity in the house, you can do a refinance to pull the cash out, thereby harvesting cash from your money tree.

The aforementioned teacher has planted 26 money trees that give her financial freedom and time freedom. MK has 20 rental properties. The husband-wife team has more than 100 active leases. Everyone's situation is different. Maybe for your case, you only need to accumulate 10 or 20 rental properties. I have read about an investor who described about her purchases of five rental houses to gradually pay off the mortgages and then retire. For her, cash-flow from five houses was enough.

The key for you is not to match their numbers, but to have enough passive cash-flow from the investments to support you and your family, without having to rely on paychecks.

Therefore, each rental property is like a "money tree". Once you have planted enough money trees, you have realized your dream of financial freedom.

Three factors will add to your financial well-being: (1) Cash-flow to enable your financial freedom, (2) further increase in cash-flow due to rent increases and paying off the mortgages over time, and (3) housing value appreciation with time to increase your net worth.

Have perspective, be grateful, be humble, and have fun. Of course, money is not everything. We need to have perspective as there are other important things in life. My wife and I came from humble beginnings, and we live frugally. China has experienced amazing developments in the past three decades. But back in the 1960s and 1970s, in my childhood, being hungry was a constant feeling. If you had asked me what heaven was like, I would have said: "Heaven is where there is plenty of food so I wouldn't be hungry, and plenty of clothes so I wouldn't be cold in the winter."

I remember that one summer, while I was middle school-aged, I walked barefoot at night in the muddy fields and creeks to catch the slippery rice-field eels. I used an oil lamp to find the eels laying in the darkness in the shallow water. After several nights, I had accumulated 1 kg of eels. The next morning, I walked about four miles to the town and sold them, for a whopping 0.64 yuan (about $0.1 USD).

While walking on the street, a lady in a store selling apples and other fruits saw that I was carrying a round bamboo container and knew that I had some money from selling the eels. She yelled at me: "You sold the eels, you have money, come buy some apples!"

I smiled and kept walking. I walked the four miles back home without spending a cent, and went straight to work. I used a knife to cut grasses in the field to feed the sheep, sweating in the nearly 100-degree weather.

One winter, my younger brother made a trap and caught a yellow weasel. My mother happily sold it at the market and used the money to buy socks for the family to endure the cold weather. Of course, we had no heating. In our small dark house that my father had built with his own hands, some windows had no glass panels while others had cracks and gaps. We had no money to install new windows. The inside of the house was almost as cold as the outside.

My wife grew up in the same village as me and had similar experiences. One of her stories was her father carrying heavy loads of mud from a drained river bottom to the rice fields for use as fertilizer. He carried these loads of about 50-60 kg each time on his shoulders till late into the night, and his pay was a sweet potato. He took that sweet potato back home to give to his pregnant and famished wife.

Mr. Deng Xiaoping re-opened the universities in China in 1977. I was lucky to go to college in 1980 after passing a national exam, being one of about ten students to go to college out of about 200 students in my high school class. In the 1980s, Mr. Deng opened the door of China to the world.

I came to the U.S. in 1988 to pursue my Ph.D. degree, supported by a scholarship from a U.S. university. Most international students came with some money in their pockets. I came with -$1500, having borrowed money to pay for my wedding in China and the airplane ticket. My wife and I had our simple wedding celebration in July and I came to the U.S. on August 5, 1988. Then she arrived the next year to join me.

A lot has changed since then. America has embraced us and educated and trained us, and has given us opportunities that we could not have imagined back then. We are truly thankful. We are immensely grateful for all the opportunities that have been given to us and all the blessings that we have received.

Due to such a humble background, my wife and I do not need a lot of money to be happy and satisfied. However, we do value freedom and independence. It means not depending on the paychecks. It means that we do not have to work if we do not want to. It means to be able to financially help family and relatives. If a family member becomes sick and needs care, we have the option to meet that need.

My dream is to retire several years earlier than usual and take my wife to travel the world. My wife dated and married me when I had nothing. In the mid-1980s, I was teaching physics in a university in China and my salary was 120 yuan/month (about $20 USD). The food in the simplest cafeteria in the university cost me 70 yuan/month. After food and other basic and minimal living expenses, it took a year's savings to buy a bike. It took a year's savings to by a wrist watch. My wife was the best student in her class, number 1 in all her exams. She's beautiful and elegant. It took a lot of courage for her to date and marry me. I have vowed to be able to take her to tour the world. By investing in real estate, the hope is that I will accomplish this dream sooner than I would just being an employee.

My other dream is to spend more time with my mother and two brothers and their families (my father passed away in December 2018). Ever since I left them in the village when I was 13 to go to a high school in the town, my times with them were limited. I came to America at the age of 23, and have missed my family in China. I would love to retire early and spend more time with them and tour the world with them.

Of course, you may have different dreams. You may dream to have the freedom to spend more time with family, relatives and friends. You may want to spend more time with your aging parents. You may be longing to spend more time with your lovely children and be able to attend their sports games, school activities, and music performances. You may want to volunteer in the community. You may want to serve in your church or your place of worship. Or you may want to pursue a hobby such as painting or dancing.

Many people have done very well in real estate. Some do big deals that amount to tens of millions or even hundreds of millions of dollars. However, for beginners, for ordinary working employees, for small investors, my humble real-life stories and small deals may be more suitable to get you started toward your financial freedom.

Read this book and other related books, start early, have the guts to pull the trigger, and have the resilience to persist in this endeavor. Practice the methods and approaches described in this book. Avoid analysis paralysis, get started, and know that practice makes perfect. Be patient and focused, and persist for 10 years or more, and your dream will come true. You will enjoy the fruits of your financial freedom, and be able to help others too, which is the focus of the next chapter.

Chapter 20. Giving Back

Service to others is the rent you pay for your room here on earth.

-- Muhammad Ali

My wife and I were watching the evening news on October 7, 2019, and saw a heart-warming scene about the 95 year-old former president Jimmy Carter. After taking a hard fall at his home and receiving 14 stitches above his eye, with a black eye and the surrounding tissues swollen, he went back the next day to participate in building a house for the poor, as a part of the Habitat for Humanity project.

Mr. Carter is the 39th U.S. president. The Jimmy & Rosalynn Carter Project has helped build numerous houses for families in need, organized by the Habitat for Humanity International. By 2018, the Carter Project had helped 4,331 families move into their houses in 14 countries. Volunteers all over the world came to build houses with Mr. Carter, totaling more than 103,000 volunteers by 2018.

It is inspiring to know that Mr. Carter is a cancer patient. He has the skin cancer metastatic melanoma, which has spread throughout his body including his brain. Having a late stage cancer, at the age of 95, he did not dwell in sadness or despair after a hard fall. Many people would be naturally worried about his or her health in such a situation. However, he fell on October 6, got 14 stiches, and the next day, he was back to building houses for the needy. This is a great country because of people like him.

Several years ago, I read an article about Bill Gates visiting China and giving a speech. And people were surprised to notice that he was wearing an old sweater with worn cuffs. However, he is the second richest person in the world with a net worth of more than $100 billion. Bill Gates and his wife have announced that they plan to give away nearly all of their money. They have so far given away nearly $45 billion through the Bill and Melinda Gates Foundation. Their work focuses on combating global poverty and human suffering. For example, they have developed vaccinations and immunizations, contributing to the nearly total eradication of the virus polio. In addition, they have been supporting efforts to eradicting malaria. They are investing in new therapies including transmission-blocking vaccines to combat malaria. Their efforts have saved millions of lives. People like them truly make the world a better place for others.

Perhaps less known is Mr. Yu Pengnian (1922 - 2015), a Hong Kong billionaire and philanthropist. He gave away all (100%) of his money to charity to help others in need (https://www.theglobeandmail.com/news/world/chinese-philanthropist-donates-it-all/article1389631/). Yu came from humble beginnings. In 1945, he worked as a rickshaw puller in

Shanghai. In the 1957, Yu went to Hong Kong and started working as a janitor.

In the 1960s, Yu was a construction worker. Later, he used his savings from his meager incomes and started to invest in properties. He eventually became a successful real estate entrepreneur. In 2008, Yu gave away one of his properties, which became the Bruce Lee Museum in Hong Kong.

Yu had suffered from poor eye sight due to cataracts. He supported student scholarships, donated for the reconstruction after the 2008 Sichuan earthquake in China, and paid for operations for those like him who suffered from cataracts who lived in villages and mountains in China and could not afford the procedure. His kindness has helped improve the quality of life for many.

These and other good examples are inspirational and uplifting. My wife and I have been serving in and donating to church, and sending money to help relatives and friends in need, especially cancer patients with very limited medical insurances.

In real estate investing, you will meet challenges when you deal with your team members, contractors, handymen, agents and tenants. The good examples will help you to keep things in perspective, be kind, and not sweat the small stuff.

There was a couple who rented one of my townhouses for a few years, then they had marriage problems and the husband, the main bread earner, moved out. The wife, with three kids, had difficulty paying the rent. She was late in payments for a while, and then she asked me to lower the rent to a level that she could afford, which I agreed. She lived there for another couple of years, and eventually moved elsewhere with her mother. There is another family in another townhouse of ours, where the main bread earner lost a job, found another job, lost it again, and found a new job, which happened several times. In the past three years, they had difficulty paying rent from time to time, and currently they still owe us about $4,000 in rent. My wife and I are fine with this as long as they are making a good effort to pay, knowing that their son is in school here and this is a very good school, and we do not want to force them out.

When you accumulate several rental properties, you will encounter situations like this. It is just statistics and probability that there will be a certain (although, small) percentage of such cases. The majority of your leases will perform well, but perhaps 5-10% of your leases will have some trouble from time to time. As long as 90% of your lease are doing well, your investing will be fine. Do not let the 5-10% that may have some difficulties scare you from investing.

Learning from the good examples helps me to be a better landlord, and it takes my stress away when faced with some challenges such as the aforementioned cases. This in turn helps me to stay positive and optimistic, and to continue to have the courage to acquire more properties. Being generous is not contradictory to being successful. In fact, many people are successful AND generous. Indeed, it would be hard for a mean and small-hearted person to be truly successful, let alone happy.

This book started with my daughter who was misdiagnosed and then was hospitalized for thee weeks with a life-threatening infection. Let me end this book with her too. She is now a fine young lady, beautiful, elegant, highly intelligent, and funny. She graduated from college, got married, and has been working in a big company. She and her husband have been serving in church, traveling, and doing rock climbing.

Seven years ago, my daughter started to support a boy in Africa through World Vision International. She was in high school and working as a waitress in a restaurant then, and every month, she sent money to support that boy, which she will continue to do until the boy reaches 18 years of age. Two years ago, she and her husband started to support a second boy through World Vision.

In March 2017, my daughter donated bone marrow to save a patient in Canada that she had never met. She learned from dkms.org that they needed bone marrow donors, and she went for a test and found that she was a match.

During the bone marrow procedure, while under general anesthesia and with her eyes closed, she uttered the words: "You can do more."

After the procedure and she woke up, the doctor asked her what she meant by "You can do more." She said: "I mean, you can take more bone marrow from me." My wife and I were in tears when we learned about this. She is our inspiration.

I wish you a happy and profitable real estate investing journey. I hope that this book is helpful to you. I hope that you will become a successful real estate investor, achieve your financial freedom, pursue your happiness, and joyfully give back in your community. I wish you all the best in your real estate investing endeavor.

Ending Remarks

Mr. Warren Buffett said that he happens to work "in an economy that rewards someone who saves lives of others on a battlefield with a medal, rewards a great teacher with thank-you notes from parents, but rewards those who can detect the mispricing of securities with sums reaching into the billions." (The Warren Buffett Way, page 3, *Robert G. Hagstrom*)

Indeed, the world's financial rewarding system is not fair. The financial payment is often not reflective of, or proportional to, the contributions.

I wrote this book to help my children learn investing, and for my friends who work really hard but have no financial freedom. This book is for the devoted teachers who get thank-you notes, for the heroes who receive medals, for the doctors and nurses and pharmacists who save lives, and for the highly-educated but lowly-paid scientific researchers.

This book is for all those who work hard but have little assets that produce passive cash-flow. Financial difficulties may be only the missing of a few paychecks away, whether due to company downsizing, recession, sickness, or the need to care for an ailing family member.

This book shows that the benefits of investing are not the birthright for Wall Street only. Small investors can achieve financial freedom through investing in real estate, with rates of return far exceeding mutual funds, as this book demonstrates.

I hope this book will help level the playing field for you.

I hope this book will help you receive a more fair share of the financial reward for your time and contributions.

I hope this book will inspire you to invest toward your financial freedom. As a result, you will have more time to pursue happiness for yourself and your loved ones.

I hope this book will help make it fairer for you so that your hard-work will receive a much better compensation. As a result, you will have the peace of mind knowing that you and your loved ones are financially secure.

Acknowledgement

I am forever grateful to my parents for raising myself and two younger brothers in China. In the midst of extreme poverty, they sent all three of us to college and paved the way for me to come to the United States for graduate school, where I was able to put down roots and start my own family. Today, China has progressed tremendously – but in the 1960s and 1970s, especially in my village, it was a difficult place to raise a family. I remember that we were hungry most of the time and walked barefoot in every season except in the dead of winter, when my mother would fashion makeshift shoes by hand, who did not have money to buy shoes from the store. My parents' hard work, perseverance, and kindness have helped mold me into who I am today.

I thank my wife for her love and support. We both have full-time jobs but she has taken the time to join and support me in my real estate ventures. She has diligently managed all the bills and recordkeeping, freeing me up to focus on searching, funding, purchasing, and management. I thank our three lovely and wonderful children; your love and support drive and inspire me, and you are part of the reasons why I wrote this book. I am also grateful to my parents-in-law for their love. Thanks also go to my son-in-law, his family, and my extended family for their kindness, and especially to my brothers and their families for their love and support. I love you all.

Heartfelt thanks go to my friend XW, who has given me tremendous help and support. Special thanks go to LK, who has kindly guided me into commercial real estate and has given me much good advice. My gratitude also goes to KK and BK for their kind support, trust and help. I'm deeply grateful to ZC, BRL, FC and CC who have given me important helps in my life. I also thank YZ for help in our loan applications and YF for help with our taxes. Thank you all so much!

Recommended Reading

Am I Being Too Subtle? The Adventures of a Business Maverick, *Sam Zell*

Buffett: The Making of an American Capitalist, *Roger Lowenstein*

Confessions of a Real Estate Entrepreneur, *James A. Randel*

Commercial Real Estate Investing, *Dolf De Roos*

Creating Wealth, *Robert Allen*

How to Get Started in Real Estate Investing, *Robert Irwin*

How to Make Money in Real Estate in the New Economy, *Matthew A. Martinez*

Investing the Templeton Way, *Lauren C. Templeton, Scott Phillips*

Money: Master the Game, *Tony Robbins*

Money Talks, Bullsh*t Walks", *Ben E. Johnson*

Real Estate Riches, *Dolf De Roos*

Rick Dad Poor Dad, *Robert T. Kiyosaki*

Street Smart, *Jim Rogers*

The Art of the Deal, *Donald J. Trump*

The Real Book of Real Estate, *Robert T. Kiyosaki*

The Snowball: Warren Buffett and the Business of Life, *Alice Schroeder*

The Warren Buffett Way, third edition, *Robert G. Hagstrom*

Two Years to a Million in Real Estate, *Matthew A. Martinez*

Unfair Advantage: The Power of Financial Education, *Robert T. Kiyosaki*

(I have learned a lot from these valuable books. Quotes from some of these books are cited and gratefully acknowledged.)

Made in the USA
Monee, IL
04 October 2020